Life Happens:
my journey through translation and other stories

conor

Alison Hughes

Alison x

Grace

Edited by Moira Bluer
Proofread by Claire Campbell

For Malcolm
You changed my life when I met you; you turned it upside down when you were taken too soon.

Acknowledgements

Many thanks to Moira for editing and Claire for proofreading my manuscript. I'm also grateful to Alina from Inbox translations for her assistance with the formatting. A special thank you to Leela Soma who has given me such invaluable advice and support.

I'd also like to thank my family, friends and colleagues who have encouraged me in the process and, above all, supported me in the last eighteen months. Some of you I have mentioned in the book, others I haven't. This in no way reflects the part you have played, and continue to play, in my life or what you mean to me. I have had to be selective in the stories I included to ensure the flow of the book. We will always have our special memories we can, and do, reminisce about when we meet in person.

***

PREFACE

How did you become a translator?

I suspect you'll have been asked this question many times and will have your own unique story to tell, especially if you entered the industry before Master's degree courses were available.

So why did I decide to tell mine? Primarily because of the events of the past two years. Nobody's life will have been left unaltered by the Covid pandemic but mine has literally been turned upside down. In parallel I've witnessed the sudden death of my husband at the age of 62 and the slow decline of my 89-year-old mum as she struggles with vascular dementia. If ever I needed a reminder to seize the moment, then this was it.

But why is my story so special? Actually, apart from my circuitous route into translation, I don't think it is. I rather hope it'll be relatable rather than extraordinary.

Those of you who are of the same 'vintage' as me will have experienced the dramatic change in the market in the early years of the 2010s. If you have young kids or even grandchildren, you'll most probably know how this can impact your time and energy. If you're translating today, you too will be facing the challenges of an even faster changing industry and possibly also the prospect of moving your business forward after Covid.

But this is not intended as a guide of any sort. It's first and foremost a story, interwoven with candid tales of my life so far and my journey through translation. There have been ups and downs, funny interludes and sensible business decisions, not to forget my travel tales (of woe) and the words of wisdom of my two beautiful grandchildren.

Working with languages can take us to many interesting places so we all have a story to tell. I hope this book will inspire others to do just that.

***

Chapter 1

LET'S START AT THE VERY BEGINNING

It's a very good place to start. Or is it? I'd prefer to set the scene on a summer's evening on the balcony of my flat in Largs. The entire sky is a brilliant orange as the sun sets on another eventful day. I look out over the water to the Isle of Cumbrae and feel very privileged to be living here. On one such evening, in contemplative mood, I started to think of the journey that had brought me to this point in my life.

Was it a lifelong dream to live in Largs? Certainly not. In fact, I spent my early childhood in a tenement flat in Glasgow before the family moved to a leafy suburb when it was time for me to go to school. I then had a very ordinary late 60s/early 70s upbringing… with a few exceptions.

My dad had two completely different jobs: not only did he run an industrial cleaning business, which he'd taken over from a great uncle, but he also co -managed a local acid folk group, The Natural Acoustic Band (NAB). The story goes that he was a member of the Round Table and the band came along to a meeting one evening looking for a manager. Never one to miss an opportunity, my dad stepped forward and, as I was recently told by Tom, one of the members, it: 'was definitely a crossroads moment in my life; that was the day everything changed for Krysia, Robin and myself- forever grateful'.

It's lovely to think that his spontaneous action had such a profound impact on the group members, who later moved to London and were signed to RCA. This also marked the beginning of his trips down south when he inevitably returned with a free *Top of the Pops* LP for my sister and me. The NAB went on to play with some famous names and at iconic music venues such as Ronnie Scott's. Sometimes dad took us with him to London and I was certainly the first of my friends to travel by plane. I can still remember the excitement of boarding a British Caledonian Airways aircraft for the first time.

Back home, we were taken to the STV studios on more than one occasion to watch the NAB record a show and we met Ralph McTell at Glasgow's City Halls when they were the support act for his UK tour. They also supported Don McLean at the Royal Albert Hall and on his UK tour, which could have been their big break. Don invited them over to the States as his support band on his US tour but the lead singer didn't want to go. She left the band shortly afterwards and that put an end to the excitement that brightened up life in 1970s suburban Glasgow. No more trips to London, no more free LPs...

Although this interlude had certainly elevated my cool credentials, I was in fact very studious and serious. The recession that began in the UK in 1973 led to my dad's business folding and our family home had to be sold. It also meant I had to move school and there was a slight problem with my favourite subject: German. At the new school, pupils started learning the language earlier and I was a full year behind.

I spent the whole summer catching up on my own so I could continue with the subject. Dedication indeed, but there was another reason for my avoiding the sun that summer. The previous year, during a holiday on the Island of Barra, I had suddenly, inexplicably, developed a severe sun allergy (more about this later). This may surprise you given Scotland's reputation for rain, but we did seem to have more hot summers back then and nobody was aware of the dangers of skin cancer. There were very few sunscreens on the market at the time and, one by one, I had become allergic to them all. Staying indoors learning German seemed like a good use of my time.

As an added bonus, keeping up the language meant I could go on a school exchange to Kassel, a city in central Germany, not far from what was then the East German border. On this, my first trip abroad, I was introduced to smoked salmon and smoked eel and thought my host family was trying to poison me. This was only one of the brand-new experiences that opened my mind to a different culture and the potential for actually using the language I was learning… if I ever plucked up the courage to speak it, that is. Sadly, like all my classmates, I spoke English for the whole trip.

By the time I was 17, I had all the qualifications I needed to pursue further education and, like most of my school friends, went to study at Glasgow University. I was also good at French, so languages were my obvious choice and, despite not doing an honours degree, I chose to take a year out as a language assistant in Germany. Because I hadn't yet found my sense of adventure, I applied to go to a school in Kassel, which I knew from my school exchange.

I wasn't posted to Kassel itself but to the Burgsitzschule in Spangenberg, a small town with around 6,000 inhabitants, situated 43km from the city. Because the town was so small, my only option for accommodation was the granny flat in the house of the Theune family.

I was the first foreign-language assistant at the school and they had no idea what to do with me. Instead of the conversation sessions I had been told to expect, they gave me classes to teach. These only filled six hours, not the contractual 12 hours I was expecting, which meant I had a lot of time to fill in a town with a beautiful castle, a few shops and not much else. When I asked for more hours, they gave me the class of an English teacher who had had a nervous breakdown (and told me it was because of her unruly pupils). I thankfully had no discipline problems, probably because I was such a novelty as the first assistant at the school.

I soon started to settle in and the Theunes included me in family events such as birthdays, christenings and even a wedding. Frau Theune and I attended baking evening classes and I was asked to join the teachers' volleyball team. It was through a teacher at volleyball practice that I was offered my first ever translation opportunity.

It so happened that the town had ties with the military band of the Royal Scots Dragoon Guards stationed in Paderborn and was about to enter an official partnership with them. Would I translate the mayor's speech for the occasion and deliver it in English on the day? Why not, I thought. I duly visited the mayor and left with his speech, which I immediately put to one side, as it was weeks until the event.

By this time I had hooked up with a university friend who had been posted to a school in Kassel and I was going up to spend weekends there, mainly drinking cognac and coke in rather dodgy nightclubs. On one such weekend, realising the partnership day was drawing close, I took the speech with me so she could help me with it on the Sunday. We'd had a particularly late and boozy night when we began the translation, armed with a pocket dictionary and nursing a raging hangover. Anything we didn't understand we just left out. The 20-minute German speech became ten in English, much to the relief of the bored soldiers on the day. Having endured the original, they were pleasantly surprised at my shorter version. Thankfully, there was no comeback from the mayor and I'm pleased to say that my translation skills have improved since then.

While I was in Spangenberg the soldiers visited several times. One of them had heard about the Scottish language assistant and one night, in the lead-up to Christmas, he decided he'd come and pay me a visit. It was 10pm and he'd been in the local *Gasthaus* all evening, so he caused quite a stir when he rang the doorbell to my granny flat downstairs, having drunkenly abandoned his car dangerously close to the Theunes' beautifully decorated outside Christmas tree. I was upstairs with the family at the time and Herr Theune ran down to answer the bell. By the time I arrived he had the poor soldier pinned against the wall. In his drunken state he managed a rather garbled explanation and was invited to visit the next day, with Frau Theune insisting I serve him coffee and some of the cream cakes we had brought home from our baking classes, while she chaperoned from the house upstairs. Nothing happened other than his face turning green at the sight of all the German cream cakes.

The Theunes often hosted another soldier, let's call him H, for reasons that will become obvious further on. I met him when he came with members of the band to entertain local pensioners at their Christmas lunch a few weeks later. I went with him to the concert and have to say I envied the pensioners who were probably already deaf. If you've heard bagpipes and drums perform in a small community hall, you'll understand what I mean.

It was my job to look after H that day, as the Theunes had been invited to a 50th wedding anniversary celebration. They left dinner and a bottle of wine for us both, which we had before going to an evening party that had been laid on for the soldiers. Several times during the evening H tried to persuade me to go back with him to the house. I just brushed off his advances and waited for the Theunes to arrive to drive us home. I'm not saying anything would have happened, but when he didn't join his bandmates on their next visit to Spangenberg, I learnt that he'd been detained at Her Majesty's pleasure for attempted murder. Life in the small town was proving to be far from uneventful, although in the early part of 1980 I didn't spend much time in Spangenberg at all.

On one occasion, an English teacher at the school invited me to spend the weekend at her flat in Kassel. On the way there, she told me one of her flatmates was away that weekend and the other was a guy who couldn't work because he'd been brain damaged in the army. Now, remember I had been living at home and then effectively moved in with a local family in a very small town. I had no experience of shared flats, and certainly not hippy ones. I can vividly remember the dirty dishes piled high in a tiny corner sink as, immediately on our arrival, I was left alone in front of the small TV screen while my colleague and her other flatmate went off to meditate. After I was served a meal (in dishes rescued from the pile), they suggested we go to visit Kassel's famous castle in the dark. I thought they meant the building; they took me into the surrounding woods, which were pitch black. They thought they were giving me an authentic visitor experience; I thought my end had come. As I clambered over tree roots and rocks, I kept remembering the flatmate's brain injury. Had they lured me here for some sort of ritual, or worse? I was mightily relieved to get back to the clapped-out car in one piece but was once again taken out of my comfort zone in a dingy bar where everyone was drinking orange juice. There was a really nice smell in the air. I had no idea what it was and simply refused the 'cigarette' that was being passed round. By the time we got back to the flat I was definitely high enough on the fumes to get an excellent night's sleep in the makeshift bed.

After this, my adventures visiting university friends who were spending their year in other parts of Germany, or in Austria or France – made possible by a 12-hour week and abundant public holidays – were pretty tame by comparison. In fact, when I met up with one friend to go youth hostelling, she was wearing velvet drainpipes and stilettos, and carrying a leather suitcase. We got some pretty funny looks as we entered the dorms. One night we arrived at an almost empty, fairly remote youth hostel. She offered to go to the shops to buy us something for dinner and I have never forgiven her for returning with a bottle of Sekt and a bar of chocolate to keep us going until breakfast the next morning.

All in all, I think I had the most interesting year of all my friends, which is ironic considering I was probably sent to the small town because I was as quiet as a mouse. I did do a lot of growing up and became more confident, although by the time I left

I was far from worldly-wise. Or maybe I just had the knack of going with the flow?

Chapter 2

ARE YOU BEING SERVED?

And go with the flow I did when, one day, as my time in Spangenberg was drawing to a close, Frau Theune asked me – totally out of the blue – if I was interested in a summer job. It turned out they had friends in Switzerland who were looking for a waitress at their small hotel in the ski resort of Disentis. With nothing planned for my return to Scotland, I decided it would be a good idea and had a phone conversation with the hotel owner, Herr Gieger, in my now pretty fluent German. Then, one Saturday morning in June I set off with all my worldly belongings packed into a single suitcase.

There was no internet or Google maps back in the day, so I only had a vague idea of where I was going from the stations where I had to change trains. It was not until I was well into my journey in Switzerland, and people were getting off the train and having snowball fights in what was ordinarily high summer, that I began to realise I was venturing into unknown territory. As we approached Disentis and people boarding the train were speaking in what sounded like Italian, I began to seriously regret my lack of research.

It turned out that they were speaking Romansch, Switzerland's fourth official language, but thankfully most locals in Disentis could also speak French and German. I was the only waitress in the small hotel, where the chefs were a lovely Romanian couple. Another minor detail: I had absolutely no waitressing experience.

It was a tough couple of months as I learnt on the job and managed to find a way to serve the elderly day-trippers who arrived on the 11.45am train each day before the 20 or so local workers came in for their set menu lunch. And, of course, after two days they expected me to remember their drinks order too. On the odd occasion, a coach party would arrive unannounced and ask if they could have lunch. When this happened, they were ushered into the function room and the family's children and their friends weren't allowed back to school until they had lined the corridor passing plates of food down to me to serve to the guests.

Another challenge was dealing with the local groups who frequently met in the bar. On one particularly busy Sunday, despite the football team giving me a hard time after their weekly practice, I managed to have a chat with a lovely couple. I later discovered from the business card left when he paid the bill, that the man was the CEO of Mumm Champagne. Herr Gieger had no interest in ordering champagne so I took the card as a souvenir, never suspecting it would play a pivotal role in my life.

The job was pretty exhausting but, with my youthful energy, I would get up at 6am on my one day off and leave on the first train out of town to explore other parts of Switzerland. I funded these trips from my generous tips because Herr Gieger was still battling Swiss bureaucracy to find a way to actually pay me a wage. When he did eventually cut through the red tape, we discovered I should have had a medical on my way into the country and obtained some papers. I'd been working illegally.

Luck was once again on my side, as the official let it pass and I received my full earnings in a lump sum. The family also paid for my air fare back to Glasgow because, despite grappling with multiple languages, including the totally incomprehensible Schwizerdütsch, dropping the odd plate and never managing to balance the money at the end of the day, I had in fact worked really hard and they wanted to show their appreciation. The Swissair flight was probably the first of my many travel 'misadventures' because I remember the air hostesses passing round Lindt chocolates to apologise for the fact the plane couldn't land for some reason.

Back home, before my final year began, I spent some of my well-earned cash on a marketing course that was being run at Glasgow University, where I met a girl called Ellen who would also have a part in shaping my future.

In my final year I studied advanced German and advanced economics and repeated second-year French, having failed both the exam and resit before going off to Germany. Second-year French was notoriously difficult to pass and German was very much my first language at the time. This, too, was about to change.

As my graduation approached, the UK was in recession and job opportunities were pretty thin on the ground. I did however manage to get two interviews when companies visited the university in search of graduate employees on what was known as the milk round. The first, for a marketing position with Ford, was an unmitigated disaster. The second, for a mail marketing company, was much more fruitful. They were looking for people for their Australian office and were interested in the fact I had lived abroad. I was called for a second interview, which was then cancelled, as they decided they didn't have the budget to take on graduates that year.

It was looking like I would graduate without a job when my dad reminded me of the business card that I had brought home from Disentis. He suggested I write to the CEO, Mr Snozzi, to ask if he had any vacancies at his champagne company. I had nothing to lose.

Not only did he reply with a lovely letter, but he offered me a choice. I could work either as a visitor guide in the cellars or as a typist/secretary in the export department. My heart was in the cellars and my head in the offices. I decided it would be good to get office experience, so the next letter I received was from one of the export directors. He was looking forward to welcoming me to the department but he wasn't sure where I would live. Perhaps I could try a hostel for migrant workers? Whatever happened, I could have a meal in the staff canteen for a few Francs each day.

 Homeless (but not hungry) was not a great prospect, so I asked a friend who spoke better French than me to phone and book me into a hotel for four nights. Flying was very expensive at the time so I set off on the sleeper to London, then continued my journey by ferry and train. This time I had at least been to the area because I'd visited a friend in Épernay during his year abroad. We'd had a really fun time, mainly visiting champagne houses for the free glass at the end of the tour, but it certainly hadn't prepared me for the adventures that lay ahead.

Chapter 3

MUMM'S THE WORD

Oh, how I envy my unflappable younger self. The faith I had in things falling into place, or rather the ability to go into situations blind with no thought for the consequences, was really quite remarkable (at times, remarkably stupid). And I often think back to my parents as they waved me off on my adventure in the days before mobile phones and computers. It probably took me a few days to figure out how to work a public phone box to let them know I had arrived safely and was fine. Well, still alive anyway.

When I woke on my first morning in Reims, I decided it would be nice to go and see Mr Snozzi to let him know I'd arrived. Looking back, I suspect that my arrival was furthermost from the mind of the CEO of a large, prestigious champagne house on a Tuesday morning. Nevertheless, I pushed open the heavy doors of Mumm Champagne S.A. and announced to the receptionist (in English, of course) that I would like to see him. She looked puzzled. Was I expected? No, I'd just come to say hello.

I was then ushered into his office. Unsurprisingly, he was rather taken aback. He did say it was nice to see me but added that he couldn't give me any special treatment. As it happened, that was the last thing on my mind but, in retrospect, just turning up at his office was tantamount to saying 'Here I am. What do I do now?'

When he found out that I hadn't sorted out anywhere to live he arranged for me to move into the Hotel Mumm, a large house adjacent to the offices, which had accommodation for seasonal tour guides on the top floor. That innocent, yet cheeky, visit to his office had paid off.

So, by the end of the week I had moved into Hotel Mumm and was sharing a flat with a Swiss girl and an English boy – both the offspring of friends of senior management – who had been working as tour guides for the summer. On the floor below us were rooms for Paris directors when they visited Reims and on the ground floor, opulent salons where receptions were held.

It was fun to have flatmates for the first few weeks, especially ones who brought back the unfinished bottles from the visitors department each evening. My initiation into champagne had begun! The English guy also had a penchant for fine red wine and would often go into town and buy a bottle to share with us in the evening. I probably drank some great wines, but the names meant absolutely nothing to me at the time and, if I'm honest, I didn't particularly enjoy them. Leaving suburban Glasgow to live in France was always going to be a culture shock, but those few weeks at Mumm were frankly quite surreal.

My initiation into office life was equally bizarre. When I arrived in the department on my first day, I was given a vacant desk and typewriter in an office occupied by seven export secretaries. There was, however, a slight – or, in the circumstances, not so slight – problem: I couldn't type. I can't remember whether the others knew this in advance. To be honest, I don't think I was ever asked the question. The solution was to give me some leaflets and tell me to practise typing the texts until I had mastered the skill. After a week of doing nothing else, I was managing a whole paragraph without getting my fingers jammed between the keys, so I was deemed 'good to go'.

I didn't graduate to dictation straight away, which was probably just as well because I couldn't do shorthand either. I debuted with letters to the bank, each one having to be typed individually on headed paper with two copies. This was done by inserting carbon paper between the original and two sheets of flimsy copy paper, one pink and one green. It was a messy business. If you made a mistake, the typewriter could correct the top copy, but you had to rub out the letters on the flimsy copies, often creating a hole. To deal with the problem, someone had spent hours punching holes in sheets of the coloured copy paper to make *gommettes,* which would be glued over the hole before the letter or word was typed again. Within weeks I was able to add chief *gommette* maker to my CV.

My colleagues were an interesting mix of young married mums and three unmarried older women. The former were kind and helpful, which was lucky given my sudden appearance in the department with absolutely no secretarial skills. The latter treated me like their little 10-year-old apprentice but also provided most of the entertainment. There were frequent dramas and amusing overreactions that passed over my head initially but did relieve the boredom of the bank letters I was typing.

Plus, there were perks. In my first week, someone came round and put a bottle of champagne on everyone's desk. Seeing my puzzled look, a colleague explained that it was a bank holiday on the Friday. I soon learnt that you didn't need much of an excuse to open a bottle.

We also had a monthly allocation of several bottles of champagne and 30 bottles of red wine, more champagne at Christmas and a few bottles for your birthday. When I arrived back at the flat one evening someone had kindly delivered the first of my bottles. By then, my flatmates had left and I was living alone at the top of the huge house. Thankfully, it didn't occur to me to just drink my way through the lot, as I might not have lived to tell this tale. I just let them pile up and took some home for Christmas. When I later mentioned my 'problem', the girls in the department helped me swap 15 of my monthly 30 bottles of red wine for water and bought some of my surplus stock.

My champagne consumption may have reduced considerably since the departure of my flatmates, but there was one glass I wasn't going to refuse. One day a wave of excitement rippled through the offices. We had been told to expect a VIP visitor. By lunchtime, the guest had arrived but we still had no idea who it was. I'd had lunch with an English girl who was a permanent member of the visitor team and she happened to know the guest was being entertained in the reception room on the ground floor of Hotel Mumm. She also happened to know the sommelier who would be serving the wine. She took me with her to the kitchen to have a sneak peek and the sommelier asked her what he should serve with the main course. Her suggested magnum of the 1973 vintage of Mumm's prestige cuvée, René Lalou, was duly opened and he poured us each a glass from the bottle before taking it in to serve the guests. It's a rather dubious claim to fame, but I'll always be able to say I've drunk champagne from the same bottle as the late ex-President Nixon.

Despite the occasional moments of excitement, however, work was pretty humdrum and I was very lonely. I'd got to know the English girl from the visitors department quite well and she had taken me along to her dance classes in the evening. Unfortunately, a few weeks later she was admitted to hospital and, as my flat was quite a bit out of town and the buses only ran until 8pm, I had no way of getting to the classes on my own. Most weekends I didn't speak to anyone from the Friday evening until the Monday morning.

As Christmas approached, I contemplated a one-way ticket back to Scotland. However, the UK was still in recession and the prospect of living at home again and looking for a job must have been even less appealing because I ended up buying a return. And thank goodness I did.

When I arrived back after the festive season Lydie, the receptionist who had ushered me into the CEO's office six months previously, struck up a conversation with me. She had noticed I was still living at Hotel Mumm so decided to tell me about the company's subsidised housing scheme. With her help, I applied for a flat that day. The flat would be unfurnished, so the next week she took me to the January sales at the local hypermarket to show me how I could buy inexpensive furniture. Never one to resist a bargain, I got carried away and bought a cooker and flatpack garden table and bench, which I decided would make good dining room furniture. It wasn't until I'd paid for them that I realised there was a problem. I didn't have a flat yet and had no access to storage. We couldn't hump them up three floors in Hotel Mumm and she had no space in her flat. Lydie, I was soon to discover, was never short of good ideas, so she asked to speak to the store manager and explained our predicament. Could he keep them in the warehouse for me until I got my flat? Unsurprisingly, the incredulous manager declined our plea. She then phoned Arlette, one of my colleagues in the export department, and asked if we could use her garage. She agreed and, of course, invited us for dinner. Within a very short time of my return to France, I had made two acquaintances who would become lifelong friends.

As it happens, we had made a very wise choice not attempting to sneak my purchases into Hotel Mumm because, when I got home that evening, I discovered that painters had arrived and erected a platform to paint the grand hallway leading to the third floor. They thought my flat was unoccupied so had left just a small square hole at the top of their ladder for them to climb through and this was my only access.

Soon afterwards, I was offered a flat through the company scheme and Lydie and I went to visit it. Despite it being rather small and at the other end of town, I accepted it because there was a bus stop nearby and it was in a beautiful setting beside the canal. Plus, it was incredibly cheap and my first major step towards freedom, or a proper social life at least, because I'd not been allowed any visitors at all at Hotel Mumm.

By now Lydie had become a firm friend and guided me through the process, helped me source more furniture and took me to pick the free wallpaper and paint that seemed to be on offer. The day I got the keys she drove me to pick up the cooker and bench set my colleague had stored in her garage, only to find she'd had fresh concrete laid on her driveway that day. Never daunted, and too excited to wait, Lydie and I climbed over a fence to access the side entrance and then lifted them back over the fence to her car.

I should point out here that French cookers, cheap ones at least, were extremely lightweight and most operated from a gas bottle. Until I got my first bottle, the cooker served as a bedside table and I slept on a second-hand sofa bed in the lounge. By this time my English friend from the visitors department had returned to work so I left poor Lydie wallpapering my flat while I returned to my dance classes.

Another explanation is required here. I was learning ballroom and Latin dancing, which was a totally normal pastime in France. If you went to a nightclub at the time, they didn't save all the slow tunes until the end of the night. There was a pattern: disco, slow, tango, waltz, rock'n'roll and back to disco. If you didn't know how to dance them all, you either embarrassed yourself or sat on the sidelines for half the night. Plus, it was fun and I made more lifelong friends at my dance classes and the Friday night dance evenings the teacher organised at a nightclub within walking distance from my flat.

Another bonus of having my own place was that I could have friends to stay. When my sister arranged to come over, I suggested meeting her at Charles de Gaulle airport and spending the night in Paris so that we could do some sightseeing the next day. Having passed through Paris but never visited the city, I had no idea where to begin looking for a hotel. My colleagues couldn't help, so I took the latest Michelin Guide from the shelf and inadvertently booked us into a hotel used by prostitutes. It looked a bit dodgy when we checked in – the girl in the shop window next to the hotel was a pretty big clue – so we went for an early dinner and headed straight back. As we went up to our room, I could understand enough of what the two German girls in the lift were saying to know they weren't in Paris to see the sights. They were in two rooms right beside ours and every hour, on the hour, we could hear the phones ringing to announce their next client. Outside, horns tooted the whole night. To this day, I'm reminded of our fateful night when I hear the introduction to the 10CC song One Night in Paris. We were dying to look out but were frightened a twitch of the curtains might be some sort of signal. We were also dying to go to the toilet but were too scared to leave our room to use the shared facilities. After a sleepless night we were, unsurprisingly, the only two guests at breakfast the next morning.

Several other friends visited over the summer. Each time, I met them in Paris and we spent the weekend there before coming back to Reims. Thankfully, a hotel recommendation from a Scottish friend spared them the 'One Night in Paris' ordeal I had endured with my sister.

As the summer of 1982 drew to a close, and my visitors had all been and gone, I decided I didn't want to spend the whole winter relying on lifts. It was time to take driving lessons. Lydie came to the rescue again and put me in touch with one of her friends who was a driving instructor.

Chapter 4

IN THE DRIVING SEAT

Now, I wasn't a complete novice, just totally useless. I'd failed three tests in the UK and had never quite thrown off the feeling that the car was in control of me. What could possibly go wrong in France? As it happens, nothing at all, if you discount the fact my instructor wasn't impressed with my first three-point turn. This had always been the one thing I was good at and I performed a perfect manoeuvre. Imagine my surprise when he told me I'd have failed my test. Why? I hadn't hit the kerb so how was the examiner to know I'd gone far enough back? (In the UK, the skill was <u>not</u> touching the kerb). He also didn't like the idea of me slowing down as we approached traffic lights. Apparently, you were meant to speed up in case they went to red. One night I was even, unexpectedly, treated to a display of his extreme driving skills when he got a phone call from his partner mid-lesson to say she'd gone into labour. Before I knew it, he'd relegated me to the passenger seat, dropped me back at my flat (thankfully) and was on his way to the hospital. I'm pleased to report he made it on time.

Before I sat the practical exam, I had to go to theory classes and pass a multiple-choice test. I saw a problem: I risked failing due to lack of vocabulary. If a sign said 'Beware of wild animals' and the question was 'If you see this sign, what do you need to look out for?' followed by a choice of four animals, I could fail if I didn't know what the animals were and which one was wild. I managed to make the point to my instructor, who arranged for a one-to-one verbal test with an examiner. I got 100% and he got his knuckles rapped, but at the end of the day it was the first confirmation that my French had improved immeasurably. In fairness, that wouldn't have been difficult because I had arrived incapable of stringing a sentence together.

The day of the practical test arrived and I passed first time. This may have been due to my perfect driving skills or, more probably, because the instructor was in the back of the car and the examiner was an old friend he hadn't seen for a while. The latter spent more time turning round to chat than he did watching what I was doing.

With a shiny new French licence in the bag, I started looking for a car. With Lydie's help once again, and advice from the concierge of Hotel Mumm, I soon became the proud owner of an Austin Mini whose previous owner had been battering it up and down the Paris/Reims motorway most weekends. With me not being a French national, it took a while for the bank to process my loan. The owner, who was probably ecstatic he had found a mug to take it off his hands, waited for the money. I gave him a bottle of champagne to thank him for his patience. I'd like to think that my generous gesture gave him at least a pang of guilt, but I rather doubt it.

Buying a British car, albeit a left-hand drive, in France was certainly not one of my best decisions.

I did have some fun with it before the problems kicked in, however.

When I picked it up after work, I drove home safely but then decided to do a very French thing. I'd drive to the boulangerie a few streets away to pick up my baguette. Now, I'd acquired the requisite skills – and a confidence on the roads I very much envy today – but I didn't have a good sense of direction. I was also unfamiliar with the one-way system close to my flat. Having successfully purchased my baguette I got completely lost on the way home and ended up at a friend's flat some distance away. She had to get in her car and lead me home. What would normally have been a five-minute walk had taken me the best part of 90 minutes.

Thankfully, I didn't repeat the experience and was soon driving to work and back. I even managed the 40km drive to Lydie's family farm in the heart of the Champagne countryside and was regularly invited to spend the weekend there. The Mini proved to be quite an attraction, as it turned out to be a racing model. Often, her brothers would take it out for a spin and Lydie and I would head off in her car to visit an aunt and uncle. Strangely, her uncle made champagne but only drank whisky. However, like all good champagne producers, he always had an open unlabelled bottle of his production in the fridge. It was duly produced and poured into tumblers for us to enjoy with homemade cakes. That beats tea and biscuits in my book!

I soon got to know the whole family and was invited to Lydie's brother's wedding. When I left work on the Friday before the big day, Reims was in the middle of a monsoon-like storm. I passed cars abandoned at the side of the road as my Mini made it through flood waters and back to the flat, which was pretty amazing given its low-lying chassis. The fact that I didn't realise you're meant to slow down in flood water may have had something to do with it. I parked it round the back of the flats because the underground car park was under a foot of water.

I was picked up the following day and spent a fabulous weekend in the country at my first French wedding. I got back on the Monday and didn't give the car a thought until the following morning. When I turned the key in the ignition, there wasn't a sound. Now, there had been a spate of engine thefts in Reims and I decided I'd become the latest victim. As I lifted the bonnet to check, a neighbour who was passing told me he had seen my car with its lights on two days previously. 'How can that be possible?' I said, 'They're not on now.' This was to be my first lesson in car mechanics.

I caught the bus to work and Lydie drove me home later that day and proceeded to remove my car battery, load it into her car and take it off to a garage to be charged. I managed to get to work the next day but couldn't get the car started to drive home. Lydie was still there and knew the Mumm handyman, who said he'd sort it out.

I'd love to tell you the full story, but it was so surreal I really can't remember exactly what happened. I know it involved him delivering the car back and, because he didn't know exactly where I lived, going off before he told me it was unsafe to drive. He also posted my keys into a mailbox 'with a foreign name' at another block of flats and I never did retrieve them.

The next morning, I saw the Mini back on the car park and used the spare keys to drive it to work, much to his alarm when he saw me arriving. He told me I'd need to nurse it to a garage and that there was only one Austin garage in Reims. It was in a part of town I'd never been to so I set off gingerly, armed with a map, and promptly got lost. I was so relieved to finally see the road that I totally missed the no-entry sign and arrived at the garage the wrong way down a one-way street. Now, what garage mechanic is going to pass up the opportunity of ripping off a blond bimbo who makes such a spectacular entrance?

There were many things wrong with my car, he told me. One was the starter motor. He said he'd fitted a new one, which failed again a week later. So it was back to the garage for him to fit another 'new' starter motor. Weeks later, the same problem occurred. It was sometimes taking me nearly a dozen attempts to get it to engage, but I was reluctant to return to the only garage in Reims that would touch a British car, so I decided to nurse it.

Then, one Saturday morning, Lydie dropped by the flat and happened to bump into the concierge. As luck would have it, she knew him because he'd previously run a garage near her parents' farm (Lydie was very quickly becoming my superhero(-ine)). And this concierge happened to know what was wrong with my car: the starter motor wasn't properly aligned, so it didn't always engage. Not only that, but he also had a solution, which he explained to me there and then. If the car didn't start, I had to get out, put my left foot on the ground (remember, it was a left-hand drive), my right foot on the clutch, put the car into gear, hold the steering wheel and jump up and down – and keep trying until the engine engaged. And this was how I started my car from then on. I did have to stop parking in prime parking spaces in the busy city centre, however, because there was inevitably a car lined up for my space and the driver didn't always appreciate having to wait, even if they did sometimes enjoy the performance.

By now it was early 1984, nearly three years since I'd arrived in France and, car problems aside, life was good. I had plenty of new friends, a great social life and lots of regular visitors from home. I also had a decent salary, regular bonuses, a subsidised flat and more champagne than I could drink, but despite it all I decided it was time to move on. I was bored at work as I was doing the same thing, day in day out, and wanted a new challenge. Several of my friends had moved to London, so I decided that would be my next destination.

Chapter 5

LONDON CALLING

It so happened that it was my job to process the annual Christmas gift requests when our agents asked us to send champagne to people they had worked with that year. This also meant there was a file containing the names and addresses of people in the wine and spirits business in the UK. One quiet afternoon in late March 1984 I took out the file and wrote down all the London addresses.

Remember Ellen, the girl I met on the marketing course? We had kept in touch and she had since moved to London, so I arranged to spend a week with her in the Easter holidays. Once that was in place, I wrote to the companies on the list to enquire about possible vacancies and tell them I'd be in London that week. Two offered me an interview.

The first was VAT 69 whisky, which was located in very posh offices on Pall Mall. I was interviewed by the General Manager and was asked to do a typing test. Now, I'd become pretty fast on a French keyboard, but the Qwerty layout proved to be a challenge. Never daunted, I did finally complete the test and a few days later I was offered the job of secretary to the General Manager and Export Director, provided I learnt shorthand. Once again, I was going to be well out of my comfort zone for a few months at least.

Although I'd decided to accept the VAT 69 offer, I did attend the interview with the second company, a wine and spirits trade magazine. In stark contrast to VAT 69, the offices were on an industrial estate outside central London. As I sat waiting for the interview (on one of the few chairs in the room that wasn't missing a part) and looked out the window onto the bleak, badly lit estate, I knew it wasn't going to be for me and was already dreading the walk back to the station. The interview did go well, and I was offered that job too, but the prospect of being in the office until 11pm on nights leading up to copy deadlines was the final nail in the coffin.

So, I left London at the end of the week with a new job and four weeks to hand in my notice, say my goodbyes, sell the car and furniture, and hand back the flat. My bosses, friends and colleagues were all quite shocked at my news, but not quite as shocked as I was when I found out I had to pay a full year's tax before I could leave the country. For some reason I hadn't noticed I'd not paid any the first year and nobody had thought to mention it. Or maybe they had and I'd just smiled and nodded? I hadn't understood much anyone had said to me in French in the first few months.

Selling the car and my furniture took on a whole new urgency. By some miracle, I found a buyer for the Mini and I sold most of my furniture to friends and colleagues. This left me with just enough to pay the tax bill, buy a ticket to London, ship the relatively few possessions I had gathered in my three years in France (mainly champagne) and pay a deposit and one month's rent.

Over in London, I was lucky that one of Ellen's housemates was happy to move closer to her work and free up her room for me. Lucky, that is, until I discovered that there were only two months left on the lease and the landlord was taking the flat off the rental market. I put that thought to the back of my mind as I prepared to start my new job and took time to find out what had been going on in the UK while I'd been away.

As an aside, back in Reims I'd had a small TV in my flat but was rarely home to watch it. I hadn't bought newspapers and it was well before the internet and 24-hour news channels, so all my updates had come from airmail letters from family and friends. In fact, I'd embarrassed myself one day when my Mumm boss had commented about my country being at war and I'd looked at him blankly. The news of the Falklands Islands invasion had still been winding its way over the Channel in a light blue airmail envelope.

After my arrival in London, I had a week to settle in before I started at VAT 69. With little else to do, and possibly a new resolution to stay up to date with current affairs, I switched on the news one day to see blue tarpaulins erected at the Libyan Embassy on St James's Square. There was a hostage situation and it all looked vaguely familiar. I was pretty sure it wasn't far from my new office.

Sure enough, the following Monday I passed the tarpaulins on the short walk from the tube station to the VAT 69 offices. It turned out that the staff in our sister company, Black & White, right next door to the Embassy, had had to escape over the roof when everything kicked off. Our canteen was in the Distillers Company building (also on St James's Square), which was boarded up, with the result that we had to sneak in the back entrance. So, from one canteen where the food had been unfamiliar and half the diners full of red wine by lunchtime, I found myself in another, adjacent to a hostage situation that was being broadcast throughout the world.

A week later, police cars went flying past our office on Pall Mall and a colleague and I watched from the Managing Director's balcony as the hostage takers were driven away from the scene. It was all over but sadly a young police officer, Yvonne Fletcher, had lost her life in the incident that had triggered the siege.

Once the distraction of the hostage situation was over, I decided I'd better start looking for a shorthand course. It was April, so any night classes at local schools were coming to an end. A small inheritance from a great-aunt meant I could afford a private school in Ealing, where I went twice a week to plug myself into an old-fashioned tape recorder and learn solo. I was tested at different speeds and think I may have achieved 70 wpm, but I never, ever used it. I relied on my own shorthand – and my memory, which was infinitely better back then – to hold down the job.

VAT 69 was a small company in a tall narrow building. It was run by a close-knit team of directors, area managers, admin staff and secretaries. Despite my lack of experience – and the fact that a friend of the Managing Director's secretary who was much better qualified than me had also interviewed for my job – I was made to feel very welcome. We were part of the larger Distillers Company Ltd, so I had lots to learn about the products and production methods of not only VAT 69 whiskies but all the Distillers Company products.

So far, so good. I'd landed on my feet in an interesting job and got on well with Ellen and her housemate, Angela, although they were busy people and rarely home. At least I'd found something to do for two nights a week, not that shorthand has ever featured top of any list for entertainment value.

We'd also started to talk about our plans for when we had to leave the house. Ellen was moving out of London, so Angela and I decided to look for somewhere together. It wasn't long before we'd found what we thought was the ideal flat, a maisonette in Harrow, and totally missed the alarm bells. The family who owned the whole house had converted the ground floor into a separate flat and moved upstairs, along with granny and their son with special needs. The landlady was a – possibly shrewd and definitely crazy – American lawyer, who told us there was someone moving into the third bedroom and we must never, ever use it. She said that our future (in reality phantom) housemate was an F1 racing driver, though he was later downgraded to a cello-playing schoolteacher. She had a great imagination if nothing else.

Then the promised washing machine never materialised and the fridge broke down. Instead of sending someone in to repair it, her husband started letting himself into our flat unannounced on the pretext that he could sort it. Things were going downhill rapidly and everything came to a head one Tuesday night.

I was not at home when it happened. Having so enjoyed learning to dance in France, I'd decided to take local ballroom dancing lessons. That evening, the only guy in the class under the age of 70 had offered me a lift home. It wasn't until we set off that I realised that Harrow had a very complicated one-way system and I didn't know my way home by car. We got hopelessly lost. It took us at least 45 minutes to do what would have been a 10-minute walk and if the guy had been hoping to try anything on that evening, driving round and round Harrow and the environs with a now-frazzled female had totally killed the mood.

I waved him an embarrassed goodbye and was met by Angela and her boyfriend desperate to tell me what I'd missed. They'd been struggling to get a signal on Angela's portable TV so had dared enter the forbidden bedroom and set it up on top of the ironing board, using a wire coat hanger as an aerial. As they settled down to watch a programme, the front door opened and our crazy landlady burst onto the scene. She had immediately known they had entered forbidden territory and Angela was told she had a week to leave the flat. Unsurprisingly, I decided to leave too.

What we didn't know, however, was that we wouldn't even last the week. In fact, when I got home from work the next day and went to put the key in the lock, I spotted a problem. The front door was gone. They'd returned the house to a family home while we were out and replaced our front door with the original glass panel. We were now living in the same house as the crazy lawyer, creepy husband, their son and her mother. I arrived on Angela's boyfriend's doorstep with my sob story and because there were no mobile phones back then, all we could do was wait for Angela to get home from work. As it happened, that wasn't until much later, as she was leaving her job that day and had gone to the pub with her colleagues to celebrate her departure. The classic cliché of not being able to put your key in the lock after a few drinks was taken to a whole new level!

My work colleagues were incredulous and, thankfully, my bosses were supportive and gave me time off to go with Angela to see Brent Council's harassment officer. This was a total waste of time, as she had too many housing problems to deal with already and had no time for two comparatively affluent girls who'd just had an unfortunate run-in with their landlady and were now missing a front door.

We moved in temporarily with Angela's boyfriend and his housemates before going on to separate flat shares. Before moving out, however, I went to Reims for a week's holiday as planned. While I was away, the stepbrother of one of the housemates visited. They'd all gone out as a group and when I asked Angela what he was like she said 'Definitely not your type'. By January 1985 I had met 'the guy who was not my type' at a party. He was called Malcolm and he asked me out. We would go on to spend the next 36 years together.

Chapter 6

[DON'T] BRING ME SUNSHINE

Malcolm had been a village postie in Wales and had requested a transfer to London for a change of scene and, above all, a bit of excitement. It was he who introduced me to culture and, ultimately, played a part in my adopting the arts as one of my specialisations many years later. We spent many a weekend in galleries, at concerts and plays, or going off to explore another city.

We rarely missed a festival and on a very hot day in the early summer of 1985 we set off for one in central London. After spending the whole day with friends, drinking chilled Red Stripe lager and listening to music, I noticed blisters had formed on all areas of exposed skin. Thankfully, I was wearing a boiler suit, which covered most of my arms and legs but my face was a mess and incredibly painful.

I knew right away what had happened, as I'd had a similar experience when I was 13 or 14. My aunt and uncle owned a croft on the Island of Barra off the west coast of Scotland and had invited me, my mum and my sister over for a holiday. I travelled ahead with my aunt and cousin and my mum brought my sister over a few days later.

The holiday got off to a bad start when a porthole fell on my head on the ferry over. We hit a storm and, undaunted and unafflicted by the seasickness that just about every other passenger seemed to be suffering, my cousin and I were enjoying watching the waves when suddenly I felt a bang on my head. The porthole we were looking through hadn't been properly secured and with one particularly big surge it had come loose and landed on top of me, hitting my cousin on the way down.

There was blood everywhere and I was eventually taken to a cabin where I could lie down. A young female crew member looked after us and the captain popped by occasionally. He was increasingly unsteady on his feet with each visit and we soon realised it wasn't the surging of the boat that was making him sway. He, like most of the adult passengers, had been drinking since we set sail.

In the midst of the mayhem, they radioed ahead for the island doctor to meet the ferry on arrival in Castlebay. Considering our ETA was 10pm on a Friday night, I'm not entirely sure the doctor was sober either and he just cleaned up the wound and – rightly or wrongly – decided I didn't need stitches (I've still got a dent in my head). The captain decided to carry me off the boat, tripped on the gangway and very nearly dropped me overboard. I'd made quite an entrance to the Island of Barra and by the next day everyone knew me as 'the girl who was hit on the head by the porthole'.

Unfortunately, that wasn't going to be the extent of my woes on that ill-fated holiday.

We had a very hot, sunny spell and one day my sister, my cousin and I set off from the croft to go to the butchers, which was actually the only shop in that part of the island at the time and stocked everything. By the time we got back, my face, arms and legs were covered in blisters. I was coated in calamine lotion and had to stay out of the sun for the rest of our stay.

The blisters didn't disappear, so I was taken to see my GP when we got home. Neither he nor his colleagues knew what it was. I was initially diagnosed with urticaria, but when it didn't clear up, he sent me for tests. I spent a week in the Western Infirmary in Glasgow before being sent up to the specialist department in Ninewells hospital in Dundee. I was indeed allergic to the sun. The solution was to use sunscreen, a rare commodity at the time. I tried the few that were available in chemists but developed an allergy to all of them in turn. The pharmacy at the Western then made me my own sunblock, a thick pink ointment that really did nothing for my street cred. I think I was probably quite relieved when, the next summer, I became allergic to that too. The family doctor suggested I try again without any protection and I was absolutely fine. In fact, I was absolutely fine for years – through my time at university and in Germany and France – until that very hot day in the early summer of 1985.

I immediately made an appointment with a local doctor, who sent me away with calamine lotion and wouldn't believe the problem was much more serious than a spot of sunburn. Eventually, my family doctor back home had to intervene and I got an emergency appointment at St John's Hospital for Diseases of the Skin. As soon as the hospital doctor saw my face, he decided to admit me. The problem was that I was in outpatients in London's Soho and the inpatients department was in Hackney. He suggested I catch the hospital minibus, which was just about to leave, but I decided I wanted to go home to collect some things and make my own way there. I left a note for Malcolm and set off on the trek over London. That night he came to visit with two friends.

Once my visitors left, I fell sound asleep. The next thing I was aware of was a nurse shaking me and shouting 'Wake up, the hospital's on fire'. I'd been so exhausted that I'd slept through the fire alarm. Unbelievably, the staff couldn't decide which door to use for evacuation and as we crossed from one side of the building to the other for a second time, I could see the smoke billowing up the stairs. It was definitely not a false alarm or even some surreal dream. Thankfully, nobody was hurt, but I learnt the next day that a patient on the male ward downstairs had set a chair on fire because he didn't like the night staff. I also discovered that I was the only patient on the ward who'd just gone back to bed and fallen asleep again afterwards.

A few days later I was sent to see a doctor, who decided I needed to go back up to outpatients to get some photos taken. She told me the hospital minibus was leaving in 10 minutes so I jumped on before it left. It wasn't until we were approaching central London that it occurred to me it might have been a good idea to have changed into some clothes first. Everyone else was dressed and I was about to hit Soho in my nightdress and dressing gown. (I have unashamedly milked this since at workshops when we've all been asked for an interesting fact about ourselves: 'I've been to Soho in my nightdress' is a great ice-breaker.) Of course, I had to wait for the return shuttle in the outpatients department while the others went to Chinatown to buy booze to take back to the ward. They'd obviously done the round trip before.

I was finally discharged after a week with a diagnosis of systemic lupus erythematosus (SLE), which I didn't investigate any further and carried on regardless. There were some advantages to the pre-internet period and my nonchalant attitude to life in my 20s because that diagnosis was downgraded to Sjögren's syndrome about eight years later. Neither disease is particularly pleasant but the latter is definitely the lesser of two evils.

I left hospital with my very own sunblock, this time a thick white cream, and arrived at the office on my first day back looking like Marcel Marceau after he'd been caught in a sandstorm. It might have been a good idea to rub it in properly and then the London grime wouldn't have stuck to it. I was also prescribed medication, which I was told could affect my eyesight and turn my skin orange. It was the now infamous Hydroxychlorine. Maybe

Trump didn't take it for Covid but to reduce his fake tan bill?

And most importantly, I had to avoid the sun whenever I could. When I was visiting a family friend Florence in Norway later that summer, this is indeed what we had intended to do when we set out in a little red boat to row across a fjord to some shops. My mum had joined me on the holiday and we'd been taken to Florence's in-laws' log cabin on a particularly hot day. The whole family was there and the men decided to go out on a uncle's boat to chop wood somewhere. I've no idea what type of shops you find on the edge of a fjord because we never made it there but my mum, who'd decided to stay behind with Florence's mother-in-law, asked me to bring back a costume doll for her friend's granddaughter.

As we set out, Florence explained that we needed to go round the coastline rather than head straight across so we wouldn't get carried away by the current. It was taking a while and I was beginning to feel bad about her doing all the rowing, so I offered to take over for a while. She asked if I'd rowed before and I said 'yes', failing to mention it had been on a boating pond in Glasgow. Big mistake.

By the time we'd swapped places we were drifting away from the coast. After a few pathetic attempts on my part to get us back on course, we had to swap over again so Florence could get us back on track. By this time we were well past the middle of the fjord and it was easier for us to make for the other side. Rowing frantically, she got us to the tiniest bay you've ever seen. It must have been about six metres square with huge cliffs behind it. This is where we spent the afternoon, under the beating sun we'd been trying to avoid.

Unbeknownst to me, and luckily for us, Florence's mother-in-law hadn't been happy about us setting out in the rowing boat in the first place. She'd kept watch on us with binoculars and as she saw the drama unfold, kept passing them to my mum and telling her something in Norwegian. My mum just smiled, took a look and thought 'That's nice, they're having a rest'.

Meanwhile, we were trying to attract attention to get rescued. We waved to a small plane but the pilot just waved back. Two boats passed and the same thing happened. Luckily, the men returned and Florence's mother-in-law sent the uncle out to tow us back with his boat. My mum came down to meet the boat as it arrived back ashore and the first thing she asked was 'Did you get the doll?'. Thankfully she'd been oblivious to the whole incident as we had been so close to being swept out into the North Sea.

We were forgiven for our exploit (eventually) and the rest of the holiday was uneventful. Then, one day we visited an English friend of Florence's and I happened to mention my frustration at being unable to speak the language. It so happened she had taught a Norwegian night class at the Polytechnic of Central London and suggested I might take lessons there. 'It's a great course,' she said, 'and they all go to the pub afterwards'. This sounded absolutely perfect.

Chapter 7

THROUGH FAIR AND FOWL

I had met Malcolm by then but, as a postman, he had an early start six mornings a week so could only socialise on weekends. I decided it would be nice for me to have something to do independently on weeknights so signed up for the Norwegian classes I had been recommended when the new term began that September. We were a diverse group studying the language for a range of reasons, mostly Norwegian other halves. Indeed, one girl had a very famous boyfriend: Morten Harket from the band a-ha, which was mega-popular at the time. She was Bunty Bailey, the girl who emerged from the comic in the video of their first hit, Take On Me.

Another class member was a Beefeater at the Tower of London and was learning the language simply because he liked Norwegians. He invited us to the tower one night after hours. We spent the evening in the bar, aptly named The Keys, with the crew of the Ark Royal, which had just docked. We saw the ceremony of the keys and went back to his flat until he politely suggested we leave before the gates closed at midnight, otherwise we'd be locked in for the night.

The class had bonded right away but, after two classes, I was disappointed that nobody had suggested the pub. The next week I took the initiative and from then on that was always our first port of call after our twice-weekly class. In fact, even if we had to skip the actual lesson for some reason, we rarely missed the meet-up afterwards. Bunty didn't come with us often, but when she did, she regaled us with tales of her days in the raunchy dance group Hot Gossip, showed us photos of her and Morten on holiday with his family and even asked our advice about a TV role she'd been offered. After a few drinks we were only too happy to give our opinion and, possibly not merely on our advice, she eventually turned it down.

Even though life in London was beginning to feel like one long party, I did have a job to go to each day. I worked hard at VAT 69 and learnt a lot about the whisky industry in the process, but looking back I realise I had the privilege of a working environment that simply doesn't exist today.

The drinks industry in the 1980s was laid back and very boozy. There were amazing perks, such as free bottles every month, long lunches and the freedom to leave the office if the occasion arose. One such occasion was the wedding of Prince Andrew and Sarah Ferguson on 23 July 1986. The secretaries headed down to The Mall to see them on their way to Westminster Abbey but returned disappointed, as the crowds had been gathering since the previous evening and visibility was poor. Never daunted, we emptied our plastic wastepaper bins and, as the happy couple returned after the ceremony, we had a grandstand view, perched head and shoulders above the crowds on our makeshift platform.

Some of the perks were a little more unusual.

It was now late 1985 and I was living in a shared house in Harrow that was owned by an American graphic designer, Jesse, who was renting out rooms in the family home while on a mission to woo back his estranged wife and kids. It was he who came to my rescue when I arrived home one Friday evening with a dead grouse.

The grouse had actually been sitting under my desk since the previous Monday morning, when the Managing Director had arrived with one each for myself and his secretary after his weekend shoot. It had obviously not occurred to him that it wouldn't be the nicest thing to be squashed up against on a crowded tube. On the Friday I decided I couldn't ignore it any longer, so I left early to avoid the rush hour.

When I got back Jesse was home and had a solution. Mrs Mac next door was Scottish, so she surely knew how to pluck a grouse. Despite his overt stereotyping, it turned out she did. My grouse was duly returned to me the next day, minus feathers and guts, in return for a bottle of VAT 69. Jesse said it now needed to be hung and promptly disappeared with it. Our paths didn't cross for a full week, during which time I had no idea it was hanging outside our bathroom window. When I was finally reunited with the poor dead animal, I invited a housemate, also called Alison, to share it with me, but our meal was cut short by a frantic Jesse who wanted to prepare 'the meal that was going to persuade his wife to return. Thankfully, he was again unsuccessful, as I'd have been homeless again.

At Christmas we were also given a huge turkey or ham. I would head back home to Scotland with my ham as hand luggage on a British Airways flight. I can't imagine them letting me travel with a 20lb ham these days and I hate to think what one of the budget airlines would make of it.

There was always a Christmas lunch in a hotel in St James's, after which the secretaries and area managers would continue to party in the marketing director's office. As we emptied his drinks cabinet after the 1985 lunch, we had absolutely no inkling of the enormity of the change that lay ahead. VAT 69 would soon be merged into the bigger United Distillers plc.

Chapter 8

A LANDMARK DECISION

Early in 1986, Guinness plc announced its takeover of Distillers Company Ltd in what was later exposed as a major corporate scandal and earned the then CEO and four of his associates a prison sentence. The company was renamed United Distillers plc in 1987 and all employees were moved from individual offices to a central building – Landmark House – in Hammersmith. As all the separate companies were effectively merging, we had to apply for newly created jobs within the organisation.

By then, I'd moved in with Malcolm in his house share and we'd decided it was as good a time as any to leave London… until the advert for three translators in a new translation department landed on my desk. I was faced with a dilemma. Should we follow our original plan or should I apply for the job? It sounded like the perfect way to escape from the secretarial work I wasn't particularly enjoying, but Malcolm had set his heart on moving out of London. And was I even qualified to work as a translator? Everything I knew about translation I'd learnt on my degree course and, even then, it had only been a tiny component among what had seemed like mounds of incomprehensible French and German literature we'd had to wade through.

We discussed the pros and cons and decided I should apply and let fate intervene, which it did a few days later when I was offered the job, without any interview or test. So that, in not exactly a nutshell, is the story of how I became a translator.

Once again, I'd been given a job I was little prepared for, so it was with great trepidation that I introduced myself to my two colleagues on my first day at Landmark House. They had both been translators at Distillers companies, one at Black & White and the other at Johnnie Walker, which didn't help my confidence, but we got along well and, after nervously asking them to take a look at my first few translations, they told me I'd be fine so I just got on with it.

Our small team came under the HR department and were initially assigned desks in the vast open-plan office on the ground floor. Having come from old buildings with a maximum of two to a room, I experienced a huge culture shock. Phones rang all the time and there was a constant flow of people in and out of the department. Apart from the general noise, it was hard to concentrate when someone nearby was having an interesting conversation. Being in the HR department, we found ourselves much more informed on staff matters than we probably should have been. Despite this 'perk', all three of us agreed it was virtually impossible to continue translating in those circumstances and asked to be moved. We were allocated a lovely little office just off the main department.

We enjoyed the autonomy and were kept pretty busy, as we provided translations for the whole building, me from French and German, and my colleagues mainly from Spanish and Portuguese. So I can't quite remember why I asked for Spanish lessons. Or why, when the language was already covered by my colleagues, my request was met with one-to-one tuition for three hours every Friday afternoon with a lovely teacher from Argentina. I think pretty much every request was granted in the 80s when tight budgets didn't exist.

After initially getting my verbs mixed up, telling her I had been drinking the TV (*beber* and *ver* are not so far apart, are they?) and that I was going to eat a dictionary that weekend (likewise, *comer* was not hugely different from *comprar*, the Spanish verb for buy), we were soon spending our time talking about everything and anything to do with whisky, marketing, the drinks industry and, of course, life in general. I didn't know then but my decision to learn Spanish would prove pivotal in a later move within the company.

A little while later, we received the very first electronic typewriter in the building. Until then we had been using manual typewriters, so imagine our excitement at being able to type a whole sentence that would appear on a tiny screen above the keyboard and could be corrected before it was committed to paper. Progress indeed.

We could be asked to translate anything from general correspondence and emails about shipments to marketing reports, letters to and from the CEO, lab reports and company accounts. Occasionally, we would also receive a phone call with a request from Guinness head office and one such request happened to arrive in really bizarre circumstances.

The night before the phone call, I had been at the Guinness Park Royal sports club. We now had access to the facilities and I had started going to kateda classes. Incidentally, this hadn't been my first choice, as I'd initially been extremely excited to see a pool on the list of activities. At the first available opportunity, a friend and I arrived on site one Saturday morning with all our swimming gear. Unable to locate the pool, we found someone in the bar who, after his initial bewilderment, finally worked out that the pool in question was actually bar pool. Unfortunately, kateda too was to be short-lived, as the discipline was banned by the martial arts association shortly after I started because of a black belt scandal. I did, however, manage to attend 10 classes or so before this happened.

On this particular evening, 15 October 1987 to be precise, a friend had come with me to the class. Because Malcolm was back home in Chester for the week, and our house was close to where she worked, she came to stay over. This was the night that the southeast of England was hit by 'the great storm of 1987' and BBC weather presenter Michael Fish became famous for saying 'Earlier on today, apparently, a woman rang the BBC and said she heard there was a hurricane on the way. Well, if you're watching, don't worry, there isn't!'

But there was and we didn't sleep a wink. The whole house shook and we could hear trees falling one after another in the street. By morning the power had failed and we arrived downstairs to an eerie silence, broken only by the sound of a battery-operated transistor radio one of my housemates had brought down to the kitchen to try to find out what exactly was happening. I did make an attempt to go to work, but the streets were deserted and the tube station closed. I was informed that the whole London tube and rail system was down, so there was nothing for it but to go back home, where I found myself alone. The others had made it to their respective jobs by bus or car.

The phone lines were still working so, having called home to reassure my parents that our house was still standing, and notified work I wouldn't be in (unsurprisingly, not many people made it to the office that day), I prepared to ride out the time until the electricity and heating came back on. In the early afternoon, the silence was broken by a phone call from the secretary of one of the top Guinness directors asking if I could translate a speech into French for him for a private event he was attending. Of course, it was urgent. In today's hi-tech world, I'd have been sent the text and expected to begin work right away. Back then, even he had to wait until I got into the office the next day.

Going back to the facilities at Park Royal. I didn't try any more activities but was really glad to have access to the company physiotherapist when my neck issues began. It all seemed to happen very quickly: I arrived at work one day in pain and by late afternoon was having trouble typing anything at all. I made an appointment with the physio and she too was puzzled. Her usual clients were guys who'd hurt their backs lugging barrels, so a desk-bound translator with what she discovered was a slipped disc, was a whole new challenge. Plus, I had no idea how I'd done it. The pain was unbelievable and I spent several nights in a chair downstairs, unable to lie down, and unable to travel to work or attempt any translation work either.

It wasn't until during one of the physio sessions that I suddenly remembered an incident that had happened on a journey to France two years previously. I had flown to Paris Charles de Gaulle and then lugged a heavy suitcase into Paris by bus. I was aware that there was a train to central Paris, but it had always seemed simpler (and cheaper) to sit on the service bus on its 90-minute journey to the Gare du Nord, via airport warehouses and some pretty dodgy suburbs, rather than find the train station, which, from memory, wasn't directly linked to the airport. Once in Paris, I had three hours to kill before my train to Reims, so I decided to go shopping. I have no idea why I didn't leave my suitcase in left luggage, but I do know that it wouldn't have had inbuilt wheels. I'd like to hope it was attached to one of the little trolleys that were available at the time, because surely even I couldn't have been stupid enough to carry a massive case crammed with clothes, toiletries and several bottles of whisky around a shopping centre? We certainly didn't travel light in these days.

Whatever the actual circumstances, I had turned to look at a rail of clothes in a shop and my neck froze. I had to nurse myself and my suitcase back to the train station and then spent the subsequent journey in agony. When my friends met me at Reims station, they were naturally concerned but decided it was nothing a few glasses of champagne couldn't sort out. Surprisingly – or maybe not? – they were right and although I woke the next morning with a hangover, my neck was absolutely fine and hadn't bothered me again until this particular incident. Since then, my neck has been my Achilles heel and I still visit a chiropractor regularly today.

Back then, Reims was my – and later mine and Malcolm's – annual holiday destination. We spent many a fun fortnight visiting different friends in the city and the nearby countryside, eating great food, drinking lots of champagne and generally unwinding from London life. Once I moved in with Malcolm, several of my French friends visited us, camping out in the living room of the house we shared with three shoe shop managers. If I could get time off work, we'd go shopping or explore the city together and, on one occasion, two of my friends and I were even treated to a private tour of the Tower of London by the Beefeater from my Norwegian class.

Malcolm was known for seeking out lesser-known parts of cities and London was no exception, so if I was at work he'd come home from his Post Office shift, have a quick shower then take our guests on one of his tours before bringing them to meet me at the office. We'd go for a drink in town and then back home for what inevitably turned into a party, with all the housemates and any other London friends who happened to be there that night.

Putting pen to paper to record my story, I'm increasingly grateful that the liver can regenerate itself. I may have missed out on a misspent youth but I certainly made up for it in my 20s. This wasn't helped by the pull of the lovely riverside pubs in Hammersmith and the fact that Landmark House had its own bar adjacent to the ninth-floor restaurant, with views right across the city. This is where our annual Christmas party was held on 21 December 1988, the night of the Lockerbie disaster.

I had arranged to travel home with a colleague who lived not far from me, but when I met her at the end of the night, she could barely stand. Despite having previously told me she didn't drink, she'd been plied with brandy all night and I had to literally manhandle her into the tube and then a taxi and put her to bed, before getting back into the waiting taxi desperate to get home and flop into a deep sleep.

Instead, I was met with Malcolm watching the horrific footage of Pan Am flight 103, which had gone down over Lockerbie. The images unfolding on our tiny portable black and white TV will stay with me forever, as will the total silence in the HR department the next morning. It turned out that one of our colleagues had waved off an American friend on the ill-fated flight, and her colleague at the next desk (both empty that day) had learnt that his ex-girlfriend had also been on board. In these days of social media, when everyone jumps on Facebook, Twitter or WhatsApp to report or follow incidents almost immediately after they occur, it's hard to convey the shock of learning the next day that something that had seemed tragic but remote on the TV screen the previous night had actually directly affected people you knew so well.

Aside from the Lockerbie tragedy, which shook the entire world, working at Landmark House was a pleasure. One of our original team had sadly left, but our new colleague fitted in well and all three of us shared the same sense of humour. We worked hard but our days were also filled with helpless laughter and, before long, my updates on the progress (or latest drama) of the plans for my forthcoming wedding.

Chapter 9

APRIL FOOLS

Yes, Malcolm had proposed. It came out of the blue and certainly wasn't traditional or romantic. In fact, I must have still looked totally shocked when I walked past workmen the following day and one shouted 'Cheer up love, it might never happen'.

Well, it did, but planning a wedding in Scotland from London was long, complicated and, as we'd find out on the day, not always adequate.

I travelled back home one weekend to make initial arrangements. The first port of call was the church in my hometown of Bearsden, outside Glasgow. We'd decided to request a date during the Easter holidays in 1989, but churches tend to be pretty busy around that time of year of course. The only Saturday available was 1st April and I took the unilateral decision that we'd be married on April Fool's Day. Malcolm wasn't quite so amenable to the date, but I eventually won him round and the planning got under way.

Neither my parents nor Malcolm's dad and stepmother had the money to lay on a wedding, so it was up to us to give our friends and family a day to remember without breaking the bank. My mum was still working at the time and her office colleagues recommended a caterer and a band.

We booked the local hall for the reception and mum and I visited the caterer, who agreed to provide a very basic meal for our budget. She also gave us the details of a bar we could book separately.

Lydie was still working for Mumm Champagne at the time and very generously offered to supply red wine from her allocation and to gift us 12 magnums of champagne as a wedding present. It would have been expensive to ship to the UK, so I decided to hold a hen weekend in Paris. That way, my French friends could join us and my UK friends could transport the wine and champagne back over the Channel. To make sure the supplies reached their destination in plenty of time, the weekend was arranged for a few months before the wedding.

After the Paris weekend fiasco with my sister back when I lived in Reims, a Scottish friend had recommended the Hotel de Milan, which was in a street halfway between the Gare du Nord and the Gare de l'Est. It wasn't fancy, but the only undesirable resident was the occasional cockroach, and I had visited often while still living in France and gone back there with Malcolm a couple of times. I decided it would be a good venue for the hen weekend, so we all booked in and the owners, a couple in their 40s, agreed to chill some champagne in their fridge and let us have a pre-dinner aperitif in the breakfast room on the Saturday night. They were lovely and very attentive, particularly the husband when his wife went out during our aperitif. He appeared from the kitchen to hand round a plate of peanuts in exchange for a glass of bubbly and the chance to join in the merriment of 20 or so very loud young women, hastily beating a retreat when his wife returned.

We moved on to a local restaurant, where things became lively when we were introduced to French drinking songs. One of my friends didn't last the pace, so I took her back to the hotel while a few of the others somehow managed to gate-crash an SNCF staff disco at the Gare du Nord. The next day was spent quietly enjoying the Paris sunshine, nursing hangovers and travelling to the airport. When we landed at Heathrow, everyone emptied the bottles of wine and champagne from their travel bags onto a luggage trolley and our precious cargo was loaded into a friend's car and taken back to her flat in Henley. It had made it across from France and would be driven up to Scotland a few days prior to the wedding.

The church, caterer and most of the drink could be ticked off the list. I arranged flowers and my mum's colleagues recommended a wedding band. One of our housemates had a camera, so he offered to be photographer, and I agreed when my dad said he could get us a cake and wedding video company through friends of his from the pub. My only instructions were to keep it simple, so I had absolutely no idea what would turn up on the day. The term bridezilla had not yet been coined in 1989, but if it had I'd have gone down in history as being the polar opposite.

I did, however, have very definite ideas about some things, such as the dresses. Well, the ones for the bridesmaids and flower girls, not really my own. That had been an impulse buy. On one of the weekends I spent in Glasgow during the initial planning phase, I'd gone shopping with my sister and found a dress I loved. It was off the peg and, if I'm honest, really a bridesmaid's dress, but I didn't want anything long or fancy and it fitted the bill perfectly.

As for the bridesmaids and flower girls, there was a slight problem: my sister lived in Glasgow, Lydie was in France, Florence's daughter was in Norway and the second flower girl was Katie, the daughter of close friends in London. How was I going to sort out the dresses? Nowadays it's trendy for them all to be slightly different, but back then they had to be the same. I hit on the idea of buying patterns and fabric and posting them out to the respective countries to be made up. We quickly agreed on and purchased the patterns, but the material proved to be more elusive, until one Thursday after work I found beautiful raw silk and lace in a very posh fabric shop on New Bond Street. The budget was blown, but my bridesmaids would look resplendent in jade green, and their little counterparts in apple green and cream.

Malcolm had asked his friend Tony to be best man and I accompanied them to a suit hire company in London. Measurements were taken and styles selected. All they had to do was try on their outfits before getting on the train to Scotland the day before the wedding. That wasn't too much to ask of them, surely? It turned out it was.

One of the last remaining items on my list was white wine and it was as I was standing at the checkout in Marks & Spencer with my trolley full of litre bottles of Soave that it occurred to me that the fridge at the hall would be too small to chill all the wine and champagne. I thought I had solved the problem by getting mum to phone the bar and ask them to bring lots of ice on the day.

As the wedding approached, I had a smaller hen do in London and, amazingly, managed to miss the second half of that too because the club was full by the time I got there, having waited for the last of my guests to leave the restaurant. One last night out was organised back in Bearsden for friends and family who'd missed London and Paris. I'd well and truly seen out my single life in style and it was time to tie the knot.

On the eve of the big day, friends and relatives started to arrive from all over the UK and also from France and Norway. Many had booked rooms in the halls of residence at a local teacher training college. I ran about like a headless chicken, making final arrangements and ensuring my guests found their accommodation. At around 7pm I returned to my parent's flat totally exhausted, ready for an early night.

On the Saturday morning, Lydie, my sister and I had an appointment with a hairdresser in Glasgow. I think he'd been recommended and I'd had one 'rehearsal' but didn't know him well, so I was slightly concerned to arrive and witness him having a major hissy fit. Someone had overbooked him and he was frantically trying to find out who it was. He ranted and raved as I nervously watched him pull my hair in all directions, unsure that he had remembered the style we'd agreed, never mind having the ability to actually recreate it in his rage. Thankfully, one of his staff members finally admitted it had been an April Fool's prank and all was well as we left the salon to drive back to Bearsden. I was starting to wonder if agreeing to the April 1st date had been a good idea after all and, as it happens, my concern was not unfounded.

Back in Milngavie, where Malcolm's dad and stepmum were booked into the same guesthouse as the groom and best man, tempers were also frayed. In their wisdom, Malcolm and Tony had collected the suits as planned but decided they would be fine, so didn't try them on. Of course, they were far from fine. Tony couldn't get his shirt fastened at the neck and Malcolm's trousers were about an inch too short. The boys swapped shirts, but there was absolutely nothing to be done about the trousers. Plus, nobody had noticed they both needed cufflinks. My future in-laws set off into the village to buy some but had no success. Their final hope was the old-fashioned Co-op, but here too the search was futile. It was a shop assistant who saved the day by going home and bringing back two pairs of her husband's for them to borrow.

All this had happened and we hadn't even made it to the church yet. Thankfully, I was blissfully unaware of what had been going on and the ceremony went off without a hitch. After a short photocall in front of the church, we set off in the car for the reception.

As I walked down the stairs to the hall I could hear the chatter of happy guests, no doubt pleased they hadn't been forced to stand around waiting for hundreds of photos to be taken and by now enjoying a glass of bubbly. I was just about to enter in search of my first glass, when I was tapped on the shoulder by the caterer. 'Are you the bride?' she asked. (Now, I know I'd chosen not to wear a proper wedding dress, but I'd have thought the veil might have provided a clue).

'Yes, I am,' I said with a smile, which quickly dissolved as I saw the concerned look on her face and she replied, 'Where's your bar?'

There had, it seemed, been crossed wires. My mum hadn't booked the bar, thinking the caterer was arranging it, and she'd simply left a message on their answer machine when she phoned about the ice. The bar had no booking and had, unsurprisingly, not followed up a request for extra ice for a wedding on April Fool's Day.

'We have plenty of wine and champagne,' I said. 'If you can just give everyone a glass, we'll think about what to do when it runs out.'

'The bar would have brought your glasses and we can't find any in the hall,' was her reply.

Now, this was definitely getting serious, but word had reached the guests and two of them kindly agreed to go to the local supermarket to buy plastic cups. I was slightly concerned about the reaction of some of my posher relatives to plastic glasses, but two elderly aunts said they'd be happy to drink out of their shoes (and that was before they'd had any wine).

In the meantime, glasses had been located in the hall, so disaster was averted and the meal could begin. But what would we do when the wine ran out? The caterer said she'd have been happy to set up a bar with her staff, but they didn't have a licence to sell alcohol. Then my dad suggested he'd go out and buy booze for everyone, at which point my mum turned a whiter shade of pale. Thankfully, Florence stepped in to save the day by asking people if they'd be happy to go over the road to the off-licence and everyone agreed. In fact, the saving grace was that there was an off-licence in the vicinity, and the manager was soon to get an unexpected bonus that evening.

One by one, groups started to make their way across the road for supplies, some emptying the fridge of German plonk, filling it with the wine they wanted to buy and returning for it later. As a result, the evening (and our wedding video) was punctuated with people carrying brown paper bags across the dance floor to their seats and happy guests working their way through bottles of decent malt instead of having to queue at a bar for measly measures. If I'd had any doubts at all about the arrangement, they were immediately dispelled when I met my elderly aunt from Barra coming out of the toilets clutching 'her own personal' litre bottle of Soave under her arm.

The band was great and played mainly 60s and 70s favourites, which, looking back, were barely retro at the time. We hadn't chosen anything in particular for the first dance, so the memorable song of the evening was New York, New York, which got everyone up on their feet and many barely sat down again. We had the obligatory Scottish country dancing (music provided by a tinny-sounding tape recorder) and the total chaos that goes with it, including Malcolm being dressed in a tartan blanket as a makeshift kilt. I had great fun dancing the rock'n'roll with my French friends (in truth, the real reason I hadn't wanted a long wedding dress) and Malcolm and I did the rounds of our guests, making sure they were all happy. Before we knew it, it was time to leave, so I phoned to order a taxi to take us to the hotel we'd booked for the night. While I was on, I checked that the minibus that had been prebooked to take our guests back to the halls of residence would definitely turn up. I was assured by the call handler that, if it had been booked, it would be there at the designated time.

The next morning we used a taxi from the same company to take us back to my parents' flat. As we got into the car, some confetti fell from the pocket of my going-away outfit.

'Were you at a wedding yesterday?' the driver asked rather sheepishly.

'Actually, we got married,' was my reply.

'Oh, you're not Iain Small's daughter, are you?'

I was indeed and he was most apologetic. This time the booking had been made, but the bus driver had – allegedly – got his dates mixed up, gone to the Rangers/Celtic game (a big event in Glasgow) the previous day, got drunk and gone home and crashed out.

Well, he'd been honest and hadn't fobbed us off with a feeble excuse, but that didn't help our guests, who'd been left stranded outside the hall. It had been panic stations at the cab office, as they'd had to redirect all their cabs back from Glasgow on a busy Saturday night. It seems our friends and family were happy to continue the party outside, but I'm not sure the local residents would have been quite as delighted.

For our honeymoon, we'd decided to hire a car and do a short tour of Stirling and the Trossachs. When I'd first arrived in London, I'd swapped my French licence for a British one, back in the pre-Brexit days when these processes were oh so simple, so I was driving. But first, we had two nights at the 5-star Gleneagles Hotel. This is not as extravagant as it sounds, because it was owned by Guinness and I was friends with the travel coordinator at Landmark House, who had got us a great deal. Malcolm, who didn't do posh, had reluctantly agreed we'd treat ourselves to one meal in the restaurant. He was later to be spared the 'agony' when I realised – as I parked our hired Austin Metro alongside the Jaguars, BMWs and Mercedes Benz in the car park – that the smart dress I'd packed for the occasion was still hanging in my mum's bedroom.

We were shown to our room – inevitably one of the smaller ones in the eaves – and got ready to go into town for dinner. We decided to walk. It was a considerable distance, but we came across a pub on the way and immediately found ourselves in the middle of a media frenzy. We gleaned from the conversations and phone calls that Princess Anne's then husband, Mark Phillips, who had a shooting school at Gleneagles, had been involved in an accident in the Philippines with another woman. The pub was packed with reporters hoping their target might be planning to take refuge at the upmarket hotel.

After one drink we continued on our way and decided to eat at a pub in town that had a decent menu. We had much to talk about, as you can imagine, but we wouldn't get any of our guests' stories about the day until we saw them again. There were no pinging phones with messages or anecdotes to share. And because of that, we didn't give it another thought. We just enjoyed the moment and the quiet meal after a hectic few days. Planning a wedding in Scotland from London had been exhausting and time-consuming and, despite the fact we had failed to tie up a few loose ends that unravelled on the day, by all accounts it seems we had given our friends a day to remember, and they still talk about it now.

We called a taxi to get back to the hotel and this was the moment we realised it was blatantly obvious that neither of us 'did posh' very well. Sitting in the back, we watched the driver take us past the grand front entrance to the staff quarters, where the chefs were standing outside having a cigarette on their break. When we told the driver we were actually guests, he tried to redeem himself by telling us that Gleneagles guests never went into town at night. This was of course true, because if you can afford to stay in a five-star hotel, you can most certainly afford to eat in the restaurant. Our mortified driver said he'd come for us the next evening and drop us at a nicer place to eat, and this is how we ended up with our own chauffeur for night two of our stay.

We left the next day and headed for Callander, where my dad had been born and brought up and I'd spent many a summer holiday staying with my grandparents (or Nanna and Pop as we called them) in the town. We'd booked a hotel for the night on the High Street. It wasn't quite Gleneagles, but we felt more at home and I was able to show Malcolm some of my childhood haunts, from the ice-cream parlour and chip shop to the Roman camp (a highlight for my Roman-obsessed husband), as well as the river and Bracklinn Falls where Pop had taken me and my sister on walks to collect leaf mould for his roses.

It was a lovely trip down memory lane, followed the next day by a stop-off in my mum's hometown (now a city) of Stirling for lunch. This trip was the first time I'd driven since I left France, but I was so much more confident behind the wheel in those days and managed to squeeze the Austin Metro into a small parking space on a hill near the castle. However, this was not France where it was acceptable to hit the car in front and the car behind gently to exit a parking space so, on our return from the restaurant, I couldn't manoeuvre the car back out onto the road. After several botched attempts Malcolm jumped out of the car and stopped a passer-by with the words 'Can you drive, mate?' The poor unsuspecting guy was handed the keys and he kindly got us out of a hole (or more accurately, a parking space).

We then returned to Bearsden for one final night before setting off by train for London, my mum insisting that we take as many of our wedding presents with us as we could pack. We reluctantly lugged the heavy suitcases back to our shared house, totally unaware that within two months they'd be winding their way back to Scotland with all our other worldly possessions.

Chapter 10

IT CAN BE GRIM UP NORTH

So why the quick departure from London? Our rental contract was due to end on 30 June 1989 and, unexpectedly, the landlord had decided not to renew it so that he could undertake some much-needed upgrades. We had two months to find somewhere else to live.

Our housemates decided to go their separate ways and we realised it was as good a time as any to make the move to Scotland. Malcolm requested a transfer through the Post Office but was told there were no opportunities. I did likewise at United Distillers and – coincidentally – the translator in the Glasgow office was expecting twins and didn't intend to come back to work after her maternity leave. Her job was mine, with one proviso. She mainly worked for the shipping department and most of the translation work was from Spanish, so I'd need to sit a test.

As I mentioned, I can't remember why I'd asked to learn Spanish while at Landmark House because I certainly didn't need it for my job. Call it providence if you will, but my Friday afternoon one-to-one lessons had paid off and I passed the test and was offered the position. However, my start date was a few weeks after we had to vacate the house.

In the interim, I moved in with good friends in Harrow and Malcolm moved up to stay with my mum and dad. As it happened, they lived beside Hillfoot sorting office, so he popped in on his first morning in Bearsden and left with a job. He started work as a delivery postman the following Monday.

When I arrived in Bearsden a few weeks later we started to flat-hunt and, in what would become our signature style, took the first one we visited. It was small but handy for my work and Malcolm could get a lift to work in the mornings from the end of the street.

The move itself had been relatively painless, but the transition from London to Glasgow was not so easy. My new colleagues were great, but the office vibe was completely different. There were no lunches in the pub and nobody took a minute more than the allotted hour. The school friends I had left behind had, understandably, forged their own lives while I had been away. Plus, it became immediately apparent that my new boss was uncomfortable managing someone from the London office. After a few cutting comments, I put him right. I may have enjoyed life in the London office to the full but no, I didn't think I was better than everyone else because I'd worked there.

Malcolm had to leave the flat at 4am six days of the week, so he was in bed by 9pm most evenings. I thought back to my Norwegian classes in London and decided to take Spanish evening classes to meet new people and, if I'm honest, quell my imposter syndrome. The experience couldn't have been more different. Everyone was friendly, but my suggestion to go for a drink afterwards fell on deaf ears. I knew I was fighting a losing battle when the teacher suggested a Christmas night out and nobody wanted to go. One woman actually said she had to get back home to make her husband's tea. So, I ended the year with no new friends but an A in my Spanish Higher (the final school exams at the time).

The night out that didn't happen coincided with a low point. I was really beginning to question why we had left London. Deep down, I knew we couldn't have afforded to continue to live there, as property prices were way beyond the scope of our joint salaries, but the lifestyle change had been brutal.

I was also in the last year of my twenties, a decade that had (mostly) been carefree and a whole lot of fun. France had been a 'coming of age' of sorts (I was definitely a late starter), and London a truly unique experience I would never repeat. Realisation hit that it was time to move on and become a sensible and responsible adult. The latter I managed though I very much doubt I'll ever truly master the 'sensible'. But let's face it, life is much more fun if you take risks and make a few rash, or as I prefer to call them intuitive, decisions.

However, my first step on the journey to maturity came before I had even reached the 30th birthday milestone when, shortly after 9am on 4 January 1990, I received a phone call from my mum at work to say that my dad had died in his sleep. He was 55.

He hadn't kept well since developing late onset type 2 diabetes and, in truth, his lifestyle had caught up with him. We were all worried about his health, but we hadn't expected him to die so suddenly. My reaction was shock, pure and simple. My sister and I spent the next few days helping mum to organise the funeral and then months helping her move on from his death. Indeed, my sister had been supporting my parents for a lot longer while I was away, so it was time for me to share the responsibilities.

Until his last few years, dad had had a good life. Before his business collapsed, he had enjoyed being his own boss and, as I mentioned earlier, co-manager of the Natural Acoustic Band. I vividly remember the first afternoon we met Tom, Robin and Krysia.

To set the scene, our house was at the very end of a cul-de-sac in a street of very houseproud wives whose husbands went out to respectable jobs and spent time with the family at the weekends. When the women got the children off to school in the morning, they would go to each other's houses for coffee… but only once they'd done the hoovering and washed the front porch. Appearances were very important.

On this particular Sunday, the band walked the full length of the road, the boys in platforms and flares and carrying their guitars and Krysia wearing a long, flowing, colourful skirt. I bet many a curtain was twitching that afternoon. Dad then asked my sister and I to get out our story books because the band was looking for a name. We were very much involved in the process and extremely disappointed that, after all the fabulous inspiration we had given them, they decided to call themselves The Natural Acoustic Band.

But this Sunday was an exception. Most others involved us all packing into dad's car to do a tour of the ongoing jobs to make sure his men had turned up for work. Why did we all go? Because mum had been at home all week. She wanted to go somewhere and anywhere, even a building site, would do. My sister and I would be reluctantly dragged away from our friends and bundled into the car to go see men cleaning a building. We were bored to tears, except for the day even we were impressed at the sneak preview of the Clyde Tunnel, as my dad's company had won the contract to clean it before it opened.

Dad was someone who did things and seized opportunities, and I like to think I've inherited this personality trait. It was he, after all, who'd suggested I follow up the business card I'd brought home from Switzerland that led to my job in Reims.

He nursed his business through the recession for as long as he could, and mum returned to the workplace as a clerical assistant with Glasgow City Council to boost income, but eventually he had to call it a day. He got a job as a security guard, we lost our house, which had been put up as collateral, and moved to a council house in a different part of Bearsden.

Dad's life changed dramatically. He was no longer the boss and had to work incredibly long shifts. He did later find a job with British Leyland that offered more reasonable hours, but his health had deteriorated. That night in January his heart had simply given up on him in his sleep.

Mum, who had never kept well, was 57 at the time and gave up work due to ill health a short time after his death.

It was around about this time that Malcolm and I decided it was time to buy our own place. We started flat-hunting a few months into 1990 and arranged to see two properties on the same night. We couldn't afford Glasgow's West End so our search took us to Maryhill, which was up and coming, or so we had heard. Thirty-two years later I can confidently say that never happened. At the time, however, we were optimistically naive and decided to make an offer on the second flat we saw that evening, which was on the market for the princely sum of £32,500. It was in an old sandstone tenement building that narrowed as it approached the main road, earning it the nickname of 'the coffin'. Our top-floor flat was spacious with magnificent views over Glasgow, so we chose to ignore – or rather believed we could live with – the inconveniencies.

I discovered one of the perils of top-floor living the hard way when I decided to bleed a radiator one evening on my return home from Spanish class. The nut flew off completely and I was left with my finger in the hole, like the Dutch boy who saved his country by putting his finger in the dyke. Unfortunately, I could see that I was going to have to do more than that to save our flat and the one below from flooding so yelled for Malcolm, who was already in bed. He held a bucket to catch the water while I panicked and phoned the fire brigade. I still get a terrible guilt trip every time I hear about unwarranted 999 calls, but, in my defence, our situation was certainly higher up the emergency scale than eating mouldy tomatoes in a sandwich, which was one of the time-wasting stories I've since heard about. They put us on to the police, who gave us the number of an emergency plumber and he thankfully saved the day, or what was left of it by that time.

And I was about to discover that living with a baby in a third floor flat without a lift was also not ideal.

Chapter 11

KEEPING IT IN THE FAMILY

Now that we had our own place, we decided to start a family, but my first pregnancy ended in a miscarriage at 12 weeks. Malcolm and I were on holiday at the time, driving round a few places in Perthshire when I realised something wasn't quite right. To complicate matters, I was driving because he didn't have a licence. We first went to the local cottage hospital in Pitlochry but were told we'd need to go to Perth Royal Infirmary. The only option was for me to drive and I was given strict instructions to call an ambulance if things got worse on the way. Thankfully, we made it, but I was told there was no heartbeat and underwent a D&C procedure.

I was lucky enough to fall pregnant again soon afterwards and this time the pregnancy went as planned. So well, in fact, that I was convinced I was going to give birth on my due date and actually had backache that day to support my theory. When the contractions didn't start, I went to bed with a hot water bottle, resigned to the fact I had been wrong, only to wake up in a pool of warm water. That's it, I thought, and jumped out of bed… to then discover the hot water bottle had burst. It was in fact to be 10 more days before Iain would arrive on 21 October 1992.

My contractions started late afternoon on the 20th but didn't progress. Malcolm went to bed early as usual and I spent a sleepless night sitting backwards on a dining room chair watching the launch of Madonna's hugely controversial book *Sex* on TV. Seductive photo after seductive photo of the American superstar was shown on the screen as I lay draped over the chair like a beached whale, springing up and walking around with each contraction. The irony didn't escape me.

When Malcolm got up for work, I decided to phone the hospital because I couldn't risk him being on his round and not being able to contact him (need I remind you that this is what happened before mobile phones?). They sent an ambulance for us and as soon as I hit the hospital bed my contractions started coming thick and fast. By early afternoon the midwife decided I was ready to go, until they discovered the baby was lying the wrong way. I had to have an epidural so he could be turned and he finally made an appearance at 4.18pm. Despite weighing only 5 lb 14 ounces/2.33 kg at 10 days late, he was absolutely fine. I, on the other hand, had a retained placenta and lost a lot of blood. It was panic stations and I remember hearing one of the doctors phoning the hospital blood bank saying, 'We need more blood, she's not stable yet'. Suffice to say, mother and son didn't enjoy that beautiful bonding moment but, in retrospect, I was lucky to have survived.

In fact, despite the incessant breast-feeding demands of a low-birthweight baby, I recovered well and was back at work three months later. I confess to going back early because life in a top-floor tenement flat with a young baby and no local friends was totally mind-numbing.

My mum watched Iain in the mornings and Malcolm would pop in and pick him up after he'd finished his round and take him home on the bus. Iain loved being with his gran and, one day when he was about 18 months, they must have been having particularly good fun because he screamed the place down and didn't want to go home. As was often the case, Malcolm was running late so had to grab him and rush him to the bus stop. The next morning when he arrived at work, he was called in by the boss to say they'd had the police at the office the previous afternoon because someone had reported a postman abducting a child. Luckily, everyone knew Iain at the post office and were able to put the officers' minds at rest. They took it no further, but perhaps it was time to move closer to mum before Malcolm got an ill-founded criminal record?

We toyed with the idea for a while and then, when winter came and I struggled to get Iain down the stairs in his heavy car seat and over the icy road to the equally treacherous car park in the morning, we decided to make the move.

Now, when I have something in mind, I generally move fast, so when I came across an advert in the Glasgow evening paper for a house in Bearsden that was being sold by Barratt under its Oak Leaf Property scheme, I phoned right away and made an appointment. Basically, Barratt builds houses and, as an incentive for existing homeowners to buy one of their new builds, they take their old property off their hands and sell it on. The house they were selling on this time wasn't in the best location, but I was very aware that our options were limited because property was so expensive in that area.

I arranged to see it on a Saturday morning when Malcolm was at work and I decided it was fine. Yes, I know, I should have learnt my lesson, but fate would play its part, thankfully. The girl told me that I could pay a deposit of £500 to reserve the house, which would be ours once we'd sold our flat. I wrote the cheque there and then and our flat went up for sale the following week. We had a few viewers, but the things that should have rung warning bells when we bought it were putting off potential buyers.

Our flat had been on the market for a few weeks when one Saturday I suggested taking my mum on a drive past the house so she could see where it was. I stopped outside and was horrified to see that someone had obviously moved in. There were curtains up and ornaments on the windowsill. I phoned the company first thing on the Monday morning, only to be told they'd taken deposit cheques from several potential buyers and the first to sell their property had got the house. They hadn't cashed the cheque but also hadn't had the decency to let us know the house wasn't ours.

A phone call to the consumer journalist at Glasgow's Evening Times only confirmed that the company was known for doing this, so I was just thankful I'd discovered the problem before we sold our own flat with expectations of moving to that house. Shortly afterwards we found a ground-floor maisonette in Milngavie, which was much better than the house we lost and our flat finally sold.

Spontaneity must be a family trait because one year, as Christmas approached, my sister suddenly had the bright idea of having a photo taken of my mum's two grandchildren at the time, her daughter Millie and Iain. She'd seen an offer somewhere for a photographer in the Debenhams store in Glasgow and at the last minute booked the final slot on a Saturday. I only had about an hour's notice to get Iain ready, so had to take some decent clothes for him out of the wash basket.

As we were driving into Glasgow with the two youngsters in the back of the car, I suddenly heard my niece saying, 'Iainie, wash your face for the photo'. Before I could stop her, Iain, who, as I mentioned earlier, had sensitive skin and was prone to eczema, had rubbed a highly scented baby wipe over his face. It immediately turned bright red and stayed that way for several hours. But that was soon to be the least of our worries when the photographer turned the handle to let us out of the studio after the shoot and it came off in his hand. We were the last people on the top floor of the massive department store, so his banging and shouting fell on deaf ears. My sister and I were laughing hysterically and nervously at the same time as the poor young guy pushed and pulled at the door to no avail. And, of course, there wasn't a phone in the studio. Thankfully, he'd arranged to meet his girlfriend, who, after waiting for a good half hour, asked to be let in to wait for him outside the studio. She didn't respond to his cries for help at first because, she said, she thought he was trying to get a particularly difficult child to pose for a photo, but finally she realised what had happened and turned the handle on the other side to let us out. I can't look at the photo of the two cousins, and Iain's scarlet face, without remembering that afternoon and being grateful the photographer had made plans for that evening.

Chapter 12

BOREDOM AND BABY NUMBER 2

Despite the odd mishap, and the burgeoning dispute with the girl upstairs over her late-night music, life was pretty uneventful and, to be honest, work was extremely dull. There really wasn't enough work for a full-time translator and I was becoming increasingly frustrated. It hadn't always been that way. When I first arrived at the Glasgow office, I'd filled my time helping out with secretarial work until a forward-thinking young manager had decided to set up an information department for the company and included me in his team. I was to provide language and cultural awareness information and I was even sent to visit British Airways in London to see the videos they had made on the topic for their business clients.

We then discovered that visitors to the offices and new starts were being shown a presentation that didn't tell them very much about the company so my boss suggested I take it over. If I remember correctly, the presentation had been delivered from an old-fashioned slide carrousel and I recreated it using an overhead projector. I interviewed each of the managers for information about their department and what it did and followed the presentation with a tour of the building. I also created a French version because we had frequent visitors from France. I was often invited to help entertain visitors in the evening and was then faced with a dilemma. After dinner, the managers and guests would settle down for a late-night session in the bar. I could join them or spend some me-time in the luxurious bedroom I had all to myself for the night. I'll let you guess which option I chose.

This was great fun while it lasted, but a new Managing Director decided the department was surplus to requirements and I ended up inputting data for a good part of my time. The gaps between translations were growing, so I volunteered to fill my spare time by coordinating sanitary certificates for the whiskies being exported to South America. Yes, that task too was as mind-numbing as it sounds.

Not only that, but the whole company was also being restructured and the atmosphere was toxic. As was common with whisky companies at the time, most people working there had gone into the business straight from school and expected to remain until retirement. Their vision of a job for life was crumbling and some who were already in their 50s had no idea what to do next. There had been a round of compulsory redundancies and a voluntary package had been put in place. By this time I was pregnant with my younger son, Matthew, and decided to take voluntary redundancy. My plan was to become a freelance translator. My boss at the time was surprised but I've repeated his words 'If anyone can do it, it's you, Alison' in my head many times at crucial moments in my subsequent freelance career.

But first, I had a baby to give birth to. I was absolutely delighted to have reached 32 weeks given that my third pregnancy had also ended in miscarriage, this time while we were visiting Malcolm's dad in Chester and involving a stay in Chester Royal Infirmary. Because of the links between Lupus and miscarriage, I was subsequently referred to a rheumatologist who happened to specialise in Sjögren's syndrome. It was he who realised that this was the autoimmune disease I had and that I'd been misdiagnosed 10 years previously in London. Thankfully, a lack of symptoms other than sun sensitivity, the non-existence of the internet and, above all, a youthful naivety had saved me from investigating or worrying about the Lupus diagnosis.

At this point, however, I still wasn't pregnant and it was a few more months before I realised that I'd finally conceived again. Malcolm, Iain and I had gone for a drive to Callander one Saturday afternoon. We arrived about lunchtime and enjoyed fish and chips in the car before locking it to go for a walk. The minute I pressed down the button in the driver's door and pushed it shut I realised the keys were still in the ignition. I'd locked us out of the car. I didn't recognise the signs at first because we were too concerned about getting back in to retrieve the keys, but absent-mindedness was often the first pregnancy symptom I experienced. I phoned the RAC, who told me it would be at least two hours. So we went to the police station to ask if they could help. Two policemen came down in a car and searched unsuccessfully for the wire coat hanger they normally carried in the boot. One of them asked me to go to The Woollen Mill, a famous shop on Callander Main Street, to ask if they had any. Unfortunately, they had switched to using plastic hangers but sent me to the dry cleaners. Aware that the policemen were waiting for my return, I ran in panting, 'Do you have a wire coat hanger? I've locked myself out of my car.' Thankfully, I didn't fit the profile of the usual car thief and they obliged. Driving home later was when I put two and two together and realised that I could possibly be pregnant. My intuition was later confirmed by a test.

Although Sjögren's syndrome is a less serious autoimmune disease, it could still cause complications in pregnancy and birth, so I was scanned every two weeks. I had been warned that the baby's heartbeat might slow down and, if this happened, he or she might have to be delivered early with a low chance of survival. Thankfully, this didn't happen, though the scans picked up that I had placenta previa, which is a low-lying placenta. I was warned that at the first sign of bleeding I had to make my way to hospital right away. Luckily, I escaped this too, but all these warnings didn't make for a carefree pregnancy.

It was, however, decided that I should go into hospital at 32 weeks as a precaution, which meant I left work on maternity leave on the Friday and was admitted to hospital the following Monday. Thankfully, Malcolm's dad had just retired and could come up and stay with Malcolm and Iain to do the nursery runs and childcare when Malcolm was at work.

When I arrived at the hospital on the Monday, I was met by the ward sister, who, despite the four-and-a-half-year gap, said, 'I think I remember you', with a nervous look on her face. It turns out she would have good reason to look so worried, though not immediately.

The prospect of six weeks in hospital was daunting but also reassuring, as both I and the baby could have been in grave danger if my placenta ruptured. Looking back, it was amazing how quickly I became institutionalised. I was always first in the queue for breakfast each morning, as – something I didn't know at the time – I had undiagnosed coeliac disease and was retaining very little nourishment for myself and the baby and was always hungry. They happened to be trialling a new buffet-type system for meals, so food was good and not in short supply. There was no shortage of entertainment either.

Back then, hospitals had smoking rooms and watching pregnant mums dragging their drip stand there for a cigarette was an eye-opener. Then there was the young girl who'd had stomach cramps on her way out clubbing with friends. She was in the bed next to me and, when the doctor was taking too long to arrive, decided she was fine and signed herself out so she and her friends could get to the club at 11pm.

95

I was put in a ward that was used for the assessment of women in early labour and the treatment of those who were admitted with problems. I was frequently kept awake at night by mums-to-be pacing up and down, watched by frantic partners. One night, a woman's partner drew the curtains and climbed into bed with her. I feared I might be in for an uncomfortable half hour until the ward sister arrived and quickly quelled any intentions he may have had of hurrying on the labour. 'I was told I could stay with her when she was in labour,' he said. 'BESIDE the bed,' the sister replied dryly.

I was being followed by a top consultant who had travelled to the US to learn how to give blood transfusions to babies in the womb for the very rare cases when mum and baby didn't have the same blood group. I got to know one of his patients pretty well, as she came in every fortnight for the procedure. I can still see her being brought back to the ward and, barely out of the general anaesthetic, literally crawling out of bed, grabbing her cigarettes and staggering along the corridor to the smoking room.

I felt safe in the hospital and was only too happy to do anything I could for myself and my unborn baby. Possibly this was because of my previous problems. To this day, I find it difficult to understand how some could puff away in the smoking room, refuse to stay in and take unnecessary risks.

Plus, I decided to put the time at my disposal to good use. I was going to be starting a business, after all, and needed to prepare. The first thing I decided to do was to buy the Glasgow Herald every day. It was the local broadsheet that every good business owner should be reading. It was also extremely dry and I struggled to read it. I did, however, find an advert for The Writers Bureau Course and decided to invest some of my redundancy money in my writing skills. An investment that has served me well in my translation business.

I passed my time well and every second day, one of two junior doctors would come to take blood from me. I'm not sure why they did this, but I'd be looking out for the doctor arriving, hoping and praying it was the confident one. He'd sit down, whip out a latex glove to use as a tourniquet and fill the syringe in seconds. My heart would sink if it was the other one, as he was absolutely hopeless. He'd position the needle several times before digging it into my vein for a very painful blood extraction experience. One day blood spurted all over my dressing gown and he said sheepishly, 'According to Good Housekeeping magazine, it'll come out if you soak it in salted water'. Was he really so bad that he'd had to research blood stain removal?

Whatever the case, I was extremely grateful that he wasn't on duty on Friday 30 May 1997. I had been told I would have a C-section and the date had been set for 4 June, which was week 37 of my pregnancy. Most C-sections took place at 38 weeks, but my consultant would be out of the country the following week and apparently the registrar didn't want to do my procedure. I can't say I felt terribly confident after hearing that.

As it happened, my body decided not to wait. On that Friday, the latest in a string of very hot days of a May heatwave, I took myself outside for a walk in the grounds for some air. Thankfully, I got back to my bed before my placenta ruptured. My first instinct was to sit on that day's Glasgow Herald to protect the sheets. Finally, I'd put it to good use!

I then pressed the buzzer and it was all systems go. The first to arrive on the scene was the confident doctor and when I noticed his hands were shaking so badly that he could barely insert the cannula, I realised the extent of the emergency. Next, a big Nigerian doctor arrived and announced, 'You're going to have your baby now, Mrs Hughes' as I succumbed to the general anaesthetic.

The next thing I knew I was barely awake holding a baby in my arms. A nurse came in and said, 'I think it's a boy'. Nobody had had the time to check. I may not have known the sex right away, but I did know that being in hospital that day could easily have saved both our lives.

Because of the bruising after the emergency C-section, I could barely move and was waited on hand and foot by the nurses. So much so that it took quite a lot of pleading from Malcolm for me to go home one week later. As it happened, once I got back to my own surroundings and sank into my own soft sofa, all my aches and pains disappeared and life slowly got back to normal.

I was now a mum of two and, with the cushion of my redundancy payment, ready to embark on a freelance career.

Chapter 13

CUTTING THE CORPORATE TIES

I left United Distillers with a promise of sorts that they would outsource their translations to me. I also had the idea that I would write to all the whisky companies in the Scotch Whisky Association and offer my services. Oh how naive I was. In truth, I'd had very little contact with the world of translation outside my in-house role. Whilst I was working in London, a savvy colleague had once arranged for the company to pay for our translation team to attend a conference run by the Institute of Translation and Interpreting [ITI] that was being held in a hotel in the city. It turns out that his was the very first conference the ITI had ever held so I suspect that I was not the only one who felt out of my depth. One of the talks was about remote working and the speaker said that translators would be working from home, or even their garden sheds, in the future. I returned to the office totally baffled about this other world, comforted that it was not one I needed to worry about. I was in a secure job, working in a great team for a big company.

But now, that world was going to be my world. I'd taken a leap of faith with very little research. I'd invested some of my redundancy money in a brand-new computer, which was sitting on a desk in the spare room, waiting for me to get started when I got home from hospital. For now, it was simply a symbol of my optimism that freelance work would be coming my way very soon.

This optimism was further fuelled by a large translation I received from a former colleague at United Distillers when Matthew was just a few weeks old. The practicalities, however, of nursing a young baby after an emergency C-section and doing a translation to a deadline were quite a different matter. I mastered the art of one-handed typing, desperately trying to find my translating brain somewhere in the new-baby fog. I delivered on time, but that translation was to be the only work I received from my former employer. The first safety net was gone in a matter of months. Thank heavens for the redundancy money, as we couldn't live on Malcolm's Post Office salary.

And that redundancy money could have been £6,000 higher had it not been for the now idle computer. When planning my maternity leave, I'd given the company a leaving date, only to subsequently discover that it would mean me losing out on state maternity benefit. The HR department had kindly reinstated me for a further two weeks (this was all academic because I was already physically in hospital), so I chose the new date to fit in with the delivery, and hence payment, of the computer. It wasn't until a lunch date with former colleagues a few months later that one of them let slip that the voluntary redundancy package had been increased from the Monday after I left. One more day and I'd have been

£6,000 richer. I felt sick, but ultimately there was nothing I could do about it. Others had found themselves in the same situation and rules were rules. Life happens and it doesn't always go your way.

On the plus side, my father-in-law, Gordon, had by now moved into his own house near to us in Milngavie so, once Iain started school, he did the school run and was then happy to look after baby Matthew for a few hours a day to let me focus on building my business. I began by writing to all the whisky companies, as planned. Letters were never left unanswered in the days before email, but the answers I received were not what I was hoping to hear. Either the company had its own translator or employed bilingual staff. In fact, United Distillers also employed linguists in account management roles, who, I later learnt, were told to do their own translations after I left, which was why that potential income stream had never materialised.

Rookie error number one: unfounded optimism.

Rookie error number two: lack of research.

It looked like I was going to have to learn the hard way. In fact, I was so ill-informed about the industry that I didn't even contact any translation agencies, though I did join the Chamber of Commerce in early 1998.

As it turned out, this wasn't such a bad idea. Once a month I would put on some smart clothes, join local entrepreneurs for lunch and feel less like a mum and more like a business owner. It was also at one of the meetings that I made contact with a local accountant I still use today and who has proved to be worth her weight in gold over the years. More about that later.

Gordon encouraged me to get out to business events, saying, 'You won't make contacts changing nappies'. As it happened, I didn't make any useful contacts at the events either, but I continued to go along to keep me focussed and, if I'm honest, for a regular dose of sanity.

Meanwhile, back at the ranch, we actually discovered that nappy-changing could be a problem in my absence. Matthew loved to watch the Teletubbies every morning. In fact, he got so excited when the programme was on that he inevitably dirtied his nappy. Gordon had only one arm so, although (amazingly) he could change wet nappies, dirty ones were a step too far. Poor Matthew was denied his favourite programme if I wasn't at home and dirty nappies would from then on be referred to as Teletubby nappies.

When I wasn't depriving my youngest of his favourite TV programme, I would take him for walks in Milngavie town centre. One afternoon I decided to pay the local Business Gateway office a visit. I awkwardly negotiated the pram through the door and asked for advice on starting a freelance translation business. Unsurprisingly, the consultant had never been asked the question before and admitted she had no idea. Then she remembered something. She disappeared and returned with a copy of the ITI Scottish Network's directory of translators and interpreters, which they had received in the post. 'It's no use to us,' she said, 'but maybe they could help you?'

I phoned the number given for the then coordinator, who asked me to fax through a copy of my CV. With great trepidation I fed the pages through the machine but was heartened by the response: 'Very impressive credentials. I'll send you an application form.'

Probably ten years on from the baffling London conference, which I'd ultimately treated as a jolly and an excuse to get out of the office, I was making contact again with the organisation that would become a cornerstone of my freelance career. The first Scottish Network (ScotNet) meeting I attended was in Edinburgh, so I even had the opportunity to travel further afield. I got a lift to that meeting and made my first contact with other freelance translators and interpreters. By the end of the day, I'd spoken to many more members of the group. Slowly but surely, I was finding my way. And, encouraged by ScotNetters, I became an associate member of ITI shortly afterwards.

What I wasn't finding, however, was much work, so I decided to sign up for the Writers Bureau course and started working my way through the modules. I was soon even earning a little from work I submitted to magazines. From short anecdotes to the letter pages [My son had a tantrum that I let run its course before asking if he was finished. He replied: I'd like to be, but my brain wants to have another one] to a double-page article about Christmas around the world for a well-known weekly magazine.

And, of course, the children were keeping me busy. As with every family, there were visits to A&E (Iain was accident-prone). The first one happened when he was about two years old. I'd made a cup of tea and, instead of placing it on a bookshelf where he might have got hold of it, I decided it would be safer to place it behind my legs. I should mention that Iain wasn't at all agile as a child. In fact, he had a terrible habit of falling flat on his face. He never learnt to put his hands out to break a fall. On this particular day he took me by surprise by running and jumping onto my lap, putting his foot right into the newly made tea. Since there were no peas in the freezer, we arrived at the hospital with a bag of frozen onion rings applied to the burn. We left with a large bandage on his foot and – waste not, want not – cooked the onion rings for dinner. It so happened I was taking him to visit friends in London the following week. So I had a toddler and a pushchair to manoeuvre onto the flight and round the tube system. If only I'd had £1 for every time someone stopped me to say he'd lost a shoe.

The next accident happened outside my mum's flat and he must have been about four because my sister was heavily pregnant with my nephew. We were visiting mum on a Saturday afternoon when Iain ran down a slope, fell flat like a domino onto a section of tiny square paving stones with sharp corners and cut his forehead badly. Luckily my sister was there and she drove us to hospital to get the wound stitched. She was a nurse, so took charge while I held his hand with my head turned away from the action, face as white as a sheet.

That wasn't the only drama involving my sister and her pregnancies. Days before she was due to give birth to her third child, my Renault 5 wouldn't start. My brother-in-law, who loves tinkering with cars and motorbikes, had a look and said the spark plugs needed changing. He'd come down and do it the next morning. Except that morning my mum phoned to tell me my sister had gone into labour. When she didn't answer the phone (only landlines back then), I assumed that she and her husband were on their way to hospital. Gordon arrived to take Matthew out for a walk in his pushchair, so I asked him to pick up some spark plugs at the local car supply shop. Little did I know that a few contractions weren't going to stop my sister and brother-in-law, who were actually in Halfords at the time buying some. When they arrived at my house shortly afterwards, I decided I needed to stop Gordon buying any more, so I phoned ahead to the car supply shop saying, 'When a man with one arm and a toddler in a pushchair comes into the shop, don't sell him spark plugs'. As Gordon pushed open the door, the owner was waiting for him. 'I've not to sell you spark plugs,' he said to an understandably baffled Gordon. This episode has been known in the family as the Monty Pythonesque spark plug story ever since. To add insult to injury, my brother-in-law was more stressed about the impending arrival than he was making out and put them in back to front. I didn't get the car going that day after all.

In fact, my brother-in-law had been trying to save me a garage bill because my redundancy money was running out by this point. Fate would intervene not long afterwards, however, when I paid my first visit to the accountant. As she was looking at our affairs she asked, 'Is it you or Malcolm who claims the married-person's allowance?' As it turned out, neither of us had been receiving it, so we submitted a claim and I was paid a much needed £1,000. That lasted us quite a while back then and, as luck would have it, I received a phone call from a contact of a former colleague in London just as it was running out.

She was working on the editorial team for English translations of France's famous Routard travel guides. Would I be interested in translating *The Routard Guide to Ireland*? The deadline must have been pretty tight because I remember my income going from virtually zero to £750 a week during the project. The English version of the guides never really took off – I later saw them in a bargain bookshop for £1 a copy – but the money was a lifesaver, and the job a turning point. Inevitably, it subsequently landed me with a huge tax bill I hadn't anticipated. Another hard lesson in the art of freelancing!

I was very fortunate that Gordon was always happy to step in and look after the boys, which enabled me to work office hours five days a week.

This kept the money coming in but was playing havoc with my health. My neck ached constantly from sitting at the computer and I began to suffer from horrible migraine-like headaches. I'd get them once a week and each one would last for 48 hours. I knew I had to do something about them.

Chapter 14

HEADACHES AND HOSPITALS

Now, when Iain was a baby, he'd had the most awful eczema. The poor wee soul was covered from head to foot and yet it never seemed to bother him, but it obviously couldn't be ignored. After creams prescribed by the doctor failed to clear it up completely, his health visitor suggested homeopathy and recommended a therapist in Glasgow. Within a few months his skin was completely clear.

I decided to visit the same homeopath for my headaches, beginning a very long journey with alternative therapies. It took a while, I had to sacrifice coffee and anything that tasted of mint, but eventually the headaches stopped. Was it the placebo effect? I'll never know, but what I do know is that the time spent discussing the ups and downs of my day-to-day life offered some sort of therapy. Unlike a doctor's appointment, when your time is limited, I had an hour with the homeopath, who was genuinely listening and pointing out potential triggers. It helped enormously.

After Matthew was born, however, I was unusually tired. I knew the tiredness that came with lack of sleep, but this was different. I was literally crawling into my own bed after reading Iain a bedtime story and dragging myself out again for night feeds. I could barely move my limbs and my lifelong stomach problems got worse. I started to lose weight and was the envy of all my new mum friends, but I knew something wasn't right. One day, as I struggled to push Matthew in his pushchair up the road to Gordon's house, I decided I'd better visit the doctor. Blood tests showed I was anaemic, so I was prescribed a course of iron pills.

They restored some of my energy, but my stomach problems persisted. It was the homeopath who suggested I might have coeliac disease. I'd never heard of it and didn't like the thought of cutting out gluten without a diagnosis. And I'd just got a new bread machine and was making fantastic, though heavily gluten-laden bread. I continued with the breadmaking, naively worsening the symptoms with every loaf.

When the time came for my annual rheumatology appointment, my routine blood tests showed that my iron was still low, as was my vitamin B and just about every other level. The consultant referred me to the gastroenterology clinic for a blood test for coeliac disease, which came back positive. I was booked for an endoscopy/biopsy to confirm the diagnosis and it so happened that on the day of the appointment, Gordon was returning to the gastro department of the same hospital for the results of a test he'd undergone a few weeks previously. He was diagnosed with stomach cancer the morning before my endoscopy. This came as a huge blow to us all because he was never ill. He'd had major problems resulting from a fall when young, leading to him losing his arm, and then a stomach ulcer in his 20s (ultimately the cause of the cancer), but since then had never had any ailments. Fortunately, the surgery to remove the tumour was a success and he recovered very quickly and didn't require any further treatment. Days after major surgery he looked healthier than I did at the time.

On my way to the hospital for my biopsy results a few weeks later, I had to brake suddenly at a roundabout and a car ran into the back of my Renault 5. That day, I ended up with whiplash in addition to my confirmed coeliac diagnosis. A personal injury claim through the insurance company was successful and I'd just received a windfall from the Nationwide Building Society, so, still having trouble moving my neck, I invested the money in chiropractic treatment. A new practice had opened locally and the results were amazing. After an initial period of 10-minute visits three times a week, I returned for a maintenance appointment every month. It was expensive, but it helped me cope with the long hours I was now spending at the computer.

My workload had increased considerably since a phone call from a former Landmark House colleague in early 1999. She told me that a US translation agency had opened its first office in London the previous year and had contacted her to ask if she'd like to work for them. She was unable to accept due to ill health but passed on my details, and I then became one of the agency's first UK-based French to English translators. They paid £50 per thousand words, a 30% weekday rush fee, a 50% premium for weekend work and, for one particularly large weekend job, the mark-up was even 100%. These were standard rates on the market at the time, so I was happy to accept as much work as I could take.

Rookie error number three: I was working virtually full-time for this agency, like an employee without the benefits.

It would be a few years before I would discover the danger of putting too many eggs in one basket and, when market conditions changed, be forced to move away from what had essentially become a comfort blanket.

In the meantime, translators had embraced technology and were now using email to receive and return jobs, and the internet to do their research. It had changed our working practices completely, and for the better, but there was a sense of impending doom as the new millennium approached. A potential error in storing and using date information (the Millennium bug) could, if not fixed, potentially cause worldwide infrastructures to crash on the stroke of midnight. Although it was unlikely that individual translators would be directly affected, the possible knock-on effect was disconcerting. There was widespread panic to update systems. It cost some companies a considerable amount of money and, conversely, proved lucrative for many IT firms.

Another sector that stood to benefit from the Millennium was hospitality, as nobody wanted to be home alone on this momentous occasion. However, many restaurants shot themselves in the foot by inflating prices and were left with unsold tickets as potential customers chose to celebrate with their families and friends instead. The boys were still young, so we broke with our habit of not marking New Year and brought in the new Millennium at a party at my sister's house.

The fireworks were spectacular, as were some hangovers, but thankfully the Millennium bug didn't add to the headaches. With a few exceptions, systems transitioned without a hitch. And once the excitement had died down, the year 2000 didn't look much different to 1999.

Chapter 15

PERIMENOPAUSE AND THE PARANORMAL

For me, however, there had been one major change. Removing gluten from my diet was not easy, but my health improved considerably. I gained weight and, more importantly, my energy was restored. In fact, I'd had to wait three months for a biopsy after the positive blood test result and, against the consultant's instructions, had already stopped eating bread and anything else that obviously contained gluten. I just didn't see the point of continuing to poison my body and, as it happened, my gut was so badly affected that he later admitted he could tell I was coeliac from the camera images alone. Switching to gluten-free bread and biscuits when there was not much else available back then wasn't easy, as the only options were provided by the NHS on prescription and were pretty awful. The real eye-opener, however, was how many other products I had to eliminate from my diet because of the hidden gluten they contained. Who'd have thought that there was gluten in sausages, English mustard and soya sauce? And in the years after my diagnosis, there were no gluten-free alternatives available.

On the plus side, however, I felt better than I had done for years and was inspired to take a step forward in my career and upgrade from associate to full membership of ITI in early 2001. There was a fast-track process on offer and, according to the information I still have on file, I simply had to submit a previous translation for assessment and a cheque for £50.

The next big move I made was in December 2002. I was at the ScotNet AGM in Edinburgh when the committee appealed for a member to take on the newly created position of events coordinator. I sat in the awkward silence that ensued telling myself that I had two young children and couldn't afford to give up much time, because I was the main breadwinner. Plus, I was fairly new to the group so couldn't possibly put myself forward. Or could I? I raised my hand – which itself took some courage because I hadn't spoken in front of everybody before – and made a suggestion: I'd find it difficult to organise events in Edinburgh, but I'd be happy to take on the role for Glasgow and the west of Scotland. Another member agreed to be my counterpart for the east and it was settled: I was now a ScotNet committee member.

As it turned out, it was my best move to date. I'd been scraping money together to attend the workshops, particularly the summer one, which involved travel and accommodation, so discovering that the committee members didn't pay annual membership dues, and that I could attend any events I organised for free, was an unexpected bonus. I also enjoyed the organisational aspect, finding venues, liaising with speakers and coordinating payments and numbers.

ScotNet meetings were sacrosanct and the summer weekend was a highlight of my year. The other meetings were, and still are, held in venues in Glasgow and Edinburgh, but the summer one is always held outside the central belt so as to be more accessible to members who live further away. The very first one I organised was a joint tourism workshop with the Media, Arts & Tourism network, which was held at a venue on the shores of Loch Lomond.

I had organised Sunday lunch on the Maid of the Loch, an old paddle steamer that was moored there and served as a restaurant. But at breakfast that morning I received a phone call from the manager to change the arrangements. I could tell the people who were staying at the same small hotel as myself, but there were others in a guest house further up the road. I'd just pop out and tell them, or so I thought… When I left the breakfast room I was met with a mass of people. It turned out there was a fun run on and my route to the guest house was packed with runners. I started to make my way through them in the opposite direction of the starting line, apologising profusely as I stepped over the outstretched limbs of bemused runners who were warming up. It wasn't until I reached the guest house and found my colleagues that I realised I should have waited until the race had started. The ScotNet members were going nowhere until the route had cleared and, if the starting whistle had been blown while I was making my way uphill, I'd have had no other option than to turn round and start running with the crowd.

This was not the first time that I'd had an incident involving the Maid of the Loch. When my sister and I were young, we were taken on a family outing on the steamer when it was still in service. The Milngavie and Bearsden Round Table had chartered it for the day to sail to somewhere on the Argyll peninsula (I can't remember the exact place), where the families were met by the local Round Table for highland games. I can still see the pipers piping us onto dry land, but my most vivid memory of the day was when the boat crashed into Balloch Pier when we arrived back at base. People and the remains of packed lunches were thrown about, but thankfully nobody was hurt.

Another memorable summer workshop was held on the Isle of Skye. A colleague and myself decided to travel there in my car and share the driving. I think we set the record for taking the longest time to cover the route, having stopped in Luss (39 miles from Glasgow) for lunch and a pleasant stroll, only to realise we still had nearly 200 miles left to travel. It took us easily eight hours to complete the journey, but it was fun and there was a whole weekend of workshops, eating, drinking, dancing and adult conversation ahead. Bliss for a working mum!

Talking of bliss, I'd also started yoga classes and our teacher's motto was 'It's not pain, it's bliss in disguise'. We tried hard to remember this as she encouraged us to twist our bodies into every position imaginable and I even managed to master the headstand. I so wished my high school gym teacher could have seen me balancing on my head and hanging from ropes on a Friday evening (she was a friend of my mum's and told her I was the stiffest pupil she'd ever taught). Apart from my new-found skills, I was amazed at my keenness to forego my Friday night wine to travel to the west end of Glasgow for my weekly yoga session.

Of course, the company helped. I travelled in with a friend and it was a small class, so we quickly bonded. Our lovely teacher was strict but put up with laughter and nonsense too. Plus, it was great therapy when I had a minor mid-life crisis. I knew exactly what was causing it: the big M! No, not big Malc (although he was lucky to survive the experience) but the menopause.

Nowadays, thanks to celebrity role models, it's become quite a topic of the moment, but 10 to 15 years ago the subject was very much taboo. I don't remember discussing it at the time with my friends either, but that may be because I entered the perimenopause in my mid-40s, so earlier than most of them. However, I do remember thinking, 'How on earth do other female translators continue to work when their brains are mush and the slightest setback is a tear-inducing drama?'

HRT wasn't an option because I also have a condition that makes me more susceptible to blood clotting, which happens to go by the name of Hughes syndrome. It wasn't of course named after me, but as syndromes go it was an odd one to add to my collection. So yoga was my only therapy and, if I'm honest, I hate to think what I'd have been like without my weekly hormone-balancing fix. I suffered badly from brain fog and irrational thoughts. The craziest was probably the idea that I'd like to go back out into the workplace. I missed paid holidays and the interaction with colleagues. I went as far as to apply for a charity job I was sure would be perfect for me but didn't even get an interview.

Undeterred, I thought more variety in my day-to-day work would be the answer, so I embarked on a new business project called Good Life Gluten Free. The idea was to provide information about gluten-free eating on a website and, on the back of this, offer my services to advise chefs on how they could make their menus more coeliac-friendly. I actually got quite far with my project. A good friend from yoga created the website, I had a logo and cards designed by Business Gateway (a Scottish organisation that provides invaluable support to new and existing business owners) and I set up an appointment with a business adviser. When the latter's first words were 'I don't know much about celeriac disease', I realised just how little people knew about the condition. Ultimately, a lack of funds stopped me from taking the venture forward and, in retrospect, even if I had made some money initially, the gluten-free trend a few years down the line saw just about every restaurant in the land jump on the bandwagon. It turned out that chefs could adapt their menus if the incentive was there, and the sound of tills ringing was all the encouragement they needed.

The moral of the story is that my foray into other ventures had convinced me that I should stick with what I was good at. And that happened to be translation. Plus, I could stlll find myself in ridiculous situations to break the monotony.

Now, some of you will think the next story was the result of menopause hormones too, but I beg to differ. When Gordon moved to his house in Milngavie, he gave us an old wardrobe he no longer wanted, which we put in the boys' room. It so happened that the previous owner of our house had had to sell up because her husband left her and they were going through a divorce. She was seriously unhappy about the situation and sadly committed suicide a few months after she moved out. I firmly believe that her soul moved into that wardrobe.

One day I went into the room and the duvet on Matthew's bed was in a hollow dome shape, as though someone was sleeping in it. Other strange things happened, but the day I found all the contents of my dressing table scattered everywhere was the point when Malcolm decided I might not be going mad and he too was freaked. But then a friend came to the rescue. She told me she'd read you could exorcise a ghost with a candle. We'd decided to get rid of the wardrobe anyway and it was outside waiting to be picked up by the council, so the following Saturday afternoon, when I was alone in the house, I lit a tealight and went into every room saying, 'I don't know who you are or where you are, but I'm taking you back to your wardrobe'. I then went outside and placed the lit tealight in the wardrobe and we were never troubled again. By that ghost anyway…

If you're still doubting my sanity, then I can back my theory with a previous incident. In general, strange things tend to happen to me around the time someone close dies. On one such occasion, in the same house, I was on the phone in the hall when a gust of wind swept past me and knocked a lightbulb from a lamp in the living room. That, I didn't imagine.

My next exploit involved my Renault 5, which was getting old and was no longer reliable, so I needed to replace it. My mum's friend Kenny said his friend's nephew had an Escort for sale. He could take us to Kilmarnock on the Sunday to have a look. So off we set, mum in the passenger seat and me and the two boys in the back. The car was perfect, but I'd need to arrange insurance. At the time, insurance offices were closed at the weekend and there were no online options.

Once I'd sorted out the policy on the Monday, we drove back to Kilmarnock to pick up the Escort. It must have been during the school holidays because both boys came with us again, as Malcolm would have been working. I handed over the cash but was really nervous about the drive back home, some 30 miles in an unfamiliar car on a route I didn't know. Luckily, I could follow Kenny, and mum said she'd come with me for moral support. But first, the car needed petrol and she said she'd pay for it to bring me luck.

We all drove into the petrol station and I was taken aback when someone came to fill up the tank, as I'd been expecting self-service. At this point, mum told me she'd had second thoughts and would be better going back with Kenny in case the boys needed anything on the journey. If that was her excuse to escape my erratic driving then it certainly backfired.

She went off to pay and meanwhile I had to negotiate this considerably bigger car round some petrol pumps to get it to the exit, where Kenny was already waiting to leave. 'That was quick,' I thought as I focussed on getting myself there, terrified they'd leave without me. I then spent a very tense hour driving behind him and breathed a sigh of relief when I parked outside the house. However, that relief was short-lived when Iain arrived at the car and announced, 'We've left gran at the petrol station'.

So, how do you leave your mum at a petrol station? Well, it turned out that mum hadn't told Kenny she'd changed her mind. While I was manoeuvring around the petrol pumps, I'd assumed she'd got into Kenny's car. He thought she was with me. It wasn't until we drew up alongside each other at a roundabout near home that Kenny noticed she was missing. But where was she now that we were back home?

Thankfully, she had her address book with her and the petrol station owner let her use the phone to call Kenny's friend. Once he managed to compose himself, the friend picked her up and took her back to his house. Kenny phoned him immediately and was relieved to find she was sitting with a brandy waiting on our call. I was a hysterical mess but saw the funny side once Kenny kindly offered to go back to collect her.

As an aside, this was only one in a long list of mum's mishaps. Most of them happened when she was on holiday with Kenny. They took Iain to Florida and in a playpark, she decided to show him that she wasn't too old to go down the slide. She gashed her arm badly and needed stitches. She was also admitted to hospital in Malta and underwent major bowel surgery. She was left on a bus in Spain when she and Kenny took my niece and nephew there for a holiday and – perhaps her most spectacular – she got bitten by one of Gibraltar's famous monkeys and required a tetanus injection. They had to stop travelling when her holiday insurance became more expensive than the holiday itself.

It seems I take after my mum in more ways than one, but most of my travel mishaps were still to come.

Chapter 16

HEATWAVE AND HORMONES

Meanwhile, in early 2003, we decided to move because I was finding it increasingly difficult to deal with our upstairs neighbour and her loud music, unruly child and constant provocation. I was trying my best to ignore her but, at the end of the day, the situation was untenable.

The housing market was booming at the time. In Scotland, properties are advertised with an 'offers over' price and potential purchasers submit bids. There would inevitably be several interested parties, so the estate agent would set a closing date and the bids received would often be 20% or more above the asking price. We were outbid on two houses before finding another ex-council house that was perfect. We pushed ourselves as far as we could go and this time, we were successful.

One of the things that attracted us to the house was the potential for a loft conversion, which we funded by selling our endowment policy, as it transpired it was no longer fit for purpose. We knew two local builders, who took on the job and agreed to do the bulk of the work in August while we were visiting friends from Reims who had since moved to Paris. Our holiday happened to coincide with the heatwave that hit Europe that summer.

The week before we left, the temperatures hit the upper 20s here in Scotland and we were already struggling, Malcolm didn't like hot weather and I had to cover up because of my allergy to the sun. I tried to stay positive, vainly hoping that the extra 10 degrees or so in France wouldn't make much difference. Oh how wrong I was.

The heat hit us as we stepped off the plane at Beauvais airport. It was like nothing we'd experienced before. Thankfully, there was air-conditioning in the coach that took us to central Paris and also in my friend Marie-Claude's car when she picked us up. The house, however, like most in the city, was not air-conditioned, so all the shutters were kept closed to keep it as cool as possible. I'd been looking forward to long lazy meals in the garden, but it was simply too hot to eat outside. We had a crash course in heatwave mitigation, something we'd never previously had to worry about having always avoided travelling outside the UK in the summer months.

Even when we went to town at 10 am the digital thermometer at the station would already be showing 40 degrees. Marie-Claude kindly drove us about in the haven of her car, where the aircon was set to 25 degrees (the temperature of an exceptionally hot summer's day in Scotland). One afternoon, she and I left our other halves at home with the boys, who were keeping cool under the lawn sprinkler, to go shopping. We got as far as Bon Marché and simply settled down on a sofa in the furniture department and spent a couple of hours catching up. Knowing how quickly you're usually approached in a Paris store if you so much as look at an item, this was totally unexpected. The heat must have even dampened the vigour of the archetypical Paris shop assistant.

We'd promised the boys a day at Disneyland Paris and couldn't disappoint them. When we set off for the park on the Thursday, the temperature had dropped to a 'mere' 36 degrees. As soon as we arrived, Malcolm, Iain and Marie-Claude set off for Thunder Mountain, as it was notoriously busy. Matthew and I joined the queue for what looked like an innocuous ride. How scary could some planes flying round a central post really be? Very scary indeed, as it turned out. The fact the ride broke down before we had reached the front of the queue did nothing to boost my dwindling confidence and then, when we finally made it into the little plane, there was no bar to hold us in place. The other three arrived back from Thunder Mountain just in time to see me holding on for dear life, screaming at Matthew not to touch the lever, while he took us up and down waving merrily to them.

On the Saturday, Marie-Claude drove us to Beauvais to catch our flight home and we were stopped by police at the entrance to the airport. Someone had flown off leaving a bag at a check-in desk and the bomb squad was on its way to blow up the offending item. We had no option but to go to the nearby McDonald's and wait for the all-clear. Luckily, Beauvais was a tiny airport at the time, so the bag was promptly disposed of and our flight left on time. After a week of extreme heat, I'd promised myself that I would never, ever complain about the Scottish weather again, a promise that was immediately forgotten when we arrived at Prestwick airport to 18 degrees.

We came home to a nearly completed loft conversion. We'd had a fabulous holiday, survived an extreme heatwave and managed to escape the worst of the dirt and dust of a renovation project to boot. All was looking good and we could soon start the finishing touches before Iain moved into his new bedroom. We had to sacrifice the third bedroom for the staircase, so I used the remaining space as my office. I also treated myself to an extra-large screen and often had to minimise it when he and his friends filed past on their way to the loft. As any translator will tell you, our research can take you down some unexpected paths.

Following on from the exceptionally hot summer, the winter of 2003/2004 was particularly icy and Malcolm fell on his round one day and ripped his Achilles tendon. He was unable to work and was finally referred to an orthopaedic consultant. The waiting time for the appointment exceeded the length of paid sick leave he was entitled to, so he had to make a decision: either return to work before the appointment or leave the Royal Mail due to ill health. In the latter case, there was a lump-sum payment on offer, which, we decided, would be a bonus and he could find a less strenuous job with more regular hours.

This turned out to be a very bad decision. He worked in a series of other jobs, ranging from cleaner to security guard and from shop assistant to carer, but none of them lasted long. Malcolm had an amazing brain that stored facts – both useful and useless – but he was not practical in the least and found it hard to adapt to a new environment. We discovered when it was too late that the Post Office had been his perfect job.

He loved being outdoors and had a wonderful relationship with his customers, most of whom lived in big houses in the leafy suburbs. He also happened to be the postman of Lord and Lady MacFarlane of Bearsden. One day he rang their doorbell to deliver a registered letter. It was Lady MacFarlane who answered and as she was signing for the letter, Malcolm spotted some paintings in the hallway that he'd seen at a recent exhibition at Kelvingrove art gallery. He told Lady MacFarlane he'd been at the exhibition and she said, 'Oh, how wonderful. Come in and see them properly'. As he was enjoying his private viewing, he mentioned that his wife worked for United Distillers (Lord MacFarlane was the chairman of the company at the time).

'What's her name?' she enquired.

Malcolm told her my name and where I worked, to which she replied, 'I must ask Norman if he knows her'. He didn't (in case you were wondering).

Another customer sent this letter to the boss of Bearsden sorting office:

Dear Sir,

I am writing on behalf of this household to express thanks for the quality of service we receive from our local postman.

We do not know his name but his efficiency and unfailing courtesy is greatly appreciated by us. In our opinion, he is an excellent ambassador for the postal service and a worthy role model for younger staff.

I do not know whether this is correct protocol but we wish to request that he be officially commended for the excellence of his manner and efficiency of service. Perhaps these views could be passed on to him as a gesture of our appreciation.

Yours sincerely,
[The customer]

It was published in the Royal Mail's national magazine with the PS: The postman is Malcolm Hughes from Bearsden delivery office.

His London colleagues will be amused by this letter, as they've since told me about some of the things he got up to at the Harrow sorting office. In fact, he also had a run-in with one of his Bearsden customers when he kicked out his leg to fend off a dog that was about to bite his ankle as the owner stood by and did nothing. In a reversal of stereotypes, she phoned the office to complain that the postman had attacked her dog. His boss called him in the next day and told him the customer was notorious for complaining. He said the best he could do was to apologise to the owner and give the dog some treats, producing a bag from the drawer in his desk. And that is how Malcolm made a doggy friend on his round.

But that was all behind him now and the pay-out didn't last as long as we'd hoped, so, reluctantly, I agreed that the new kitchen would have to be put on hold... until fate intervened. The existing one had been installed when the house was built in the 1950s. I'd convinced myself that it had a lovely retro charm and piled crockery into the only wall cupboard, utilising the space above it to store different gadgets. Then, one Saturday afternoon I walked into the kitchen and the whole lot collapsed, thankfully narrowly missing me, although I did end up having to get medical treatment for a badly gashed thumb. The boys heard the crash from two floors up in the loft and came rushing down to find out what had happened. I was standing dazed in the kitchen surrounded by broken crockery and a cupboard in pieces on the floor. The two solitary nails that had been holding it to the wall had given up under the weight of 21st century paraphernalia.

Not long after the incident, I was sent for a neck X-ray and it was a locum doctor who delivered the result. She already had a morose demeanour so her announcement that 'I don't know what to tell you' frightened the life out of me. She then pointed to a spot on the X-ray and said, 'I have absolutely no idea what that is'. My suggestion that a bone could have been chipped when my kitchen cupboard fell off the wall perplexed her even further and we both finally agreed that it had probably been a spot of dirt on the X-ray machine.

By now we're halfway through the first decade of the 21st century and my mind has gone blank. I either have a gap in my memory or the next five years were genuinely rather uneventful. Or as uneventful as a life can be with a teenager in the house.

In 2006, Iain turned 14 and was old enough for his first job, which was delivering the free newspaper every Saturday. They'd be dropped off on the Friday and by the time I got home from shopping on Saturday lunchtime they had – Iain always told me – been delivered. 'How did you do it so quickly?' I'd ask. 'A friend helped me,' was his reply.

This little ruse was working well with his gullible mum until the father of one of Matthew's friends came to pick him up after a play date. He saw the pile in the hall and said, 'Oh, we haven't had a free paper for months'. I happened to know that they lived on Iain's round, so when he left, I went up to the loft and discovered piles and piles of free newspapers in the cupboard. Quite apart from it being a fire hazard, he'd been getting money under false pretences. This is probably the only time that I really lost it with him. He was ordered to start delivering them again, but I was confiscating his bank card and giving the money to charity.

But what to do with all those newspapers? I was absolutely furious, but I didn't want Iain to get into trouble with the company, so I decided I couldn't dispose of them all at once. What if the person emptying the bin reported the discovery and they were traced back to him? This was totally irrational, of course, but the next few Saturdays saw me sneaking as many as I could into the car boot and driving round different supermarket recycling centres attempting to dispose of them without being seen. I could only have looked more ridiculous if I'd worn a wig and a false moustache.

As you might surmise, I'm not good at breaking rules, so when I inadvertently bought a stolen mattress a couple of years later, I worried about it for weeks afterwards. It was a Wednesday afternoon and I noticed we'd run out of milk. When I got to the local corner shop, there was a white van outside and the driver approached me. Was I interested in buying a brand-new mattress? Well, as it happened, the mattress on our bed was really old. He went on to say that he'd just finished a hotel refit and his boss told him he could have the surplus mattresses to sell on by way of a bonus. Perfect, I thought. How much? £250 sounded a good price, so the van followed me round to our house and the guy and his young son proceeded to carry the mattress up to the bedroom, watched by a bemused Malcolm.

'It's ok,' I reassured him. 'It's bona fide and they're going to give me a receipt.'

Which they did in the name of a completely fictitious company. As several people on the estate had bought one (or so they told me), when I discovered I'd been duped – although in fairness we had a lovely new mattress for a bargain price – I got it into my head that the police would come knocking at the door. If everyone on the estate who'd made a purchase phoned the council to have their old mattress uplifted, we'd be easy to trace. It was weeks before I let Malcolm phone to organise the uplift. Of course, I'd probably been the only one gullible enough to buy their story and had nothing whatsoever to fear.

Mid-life hormones have a lot to answer for. As I approached my half-century, I was hoping for more sanity but life threw some curveballs in my way.

Chapter 17

THE ART OF VOLUNTEERING

The new decade got off to an inauspicious start when, on a Thursday morning in late March 2010, I received a phone call from Gordon to tell me he had blood in his urine. Unlike most men who stick their head in the sand at the slightest hint of a medical issue, he'd been on the doorstep waiting for the doctors' surgery to open and had an appointment for later that day. The doctor referred him to urology and I took him to an outpatients' appointment a few weeks later. They conducted tests, which revealed he had a cancerous tumour on his kidney. We were reassured that he'd had a CT scan and the cancer hadn't spread, so they would simply operate to remove the tumour.

Unfortunately, he wasn't so lucky this time. He was booked in for his pre-op check on 14 April, my 50th birthday. As this was a routine procedure, I didn't go with him because Malcolm and I had booked for an exhibition at Kelvingrove art gallery. The family was coming round for a mini-celebration that evening.

When we arrived back at the house, however, Gordon phoned to say his chest X-ray had revealed multiple lesions on his lungs. They hadn't done a full-body CT scan before reassuring us that the cancer hadn't spread. Suffice to say that my

50th birthday celebration was very subdued, as was the family trip on the West Highland line I had booked for us the next day. We were all worried about what lay ahead.

Gordon's original operation was cancelled and he received chemotherapy instead. I drove him to the hospital for his infusion every two weeks and between visits he had to take chemo tablets, which was an alien concept for a man who'd barely swallowed a paracetamol in his life. He coped well and continued to come for dinner on a Sunday evening, washing down his last tablet of the day with a gin and tonic or a glass of wine. He walked home every week, refusing point-blank to call a taxi.

In the November, when he was having his second round of chemo, Scotland was hit by a freak cold spell. Almost a foot of snow fell very quickly, which was in itself unusual. However, in the West of Scotland the snow doesn't normally last so most people didn't clear it away. Pavements and paths were still covered in deep snow when temperatures plummeted on the first night and stayed well below zero for six weeks. Venturing out was treacherous and yet Gordon still insisted on coming for dinner and walking home again. He only later admitted he'd been holding on to hedges, walls and fences trying to stay on his feet. He was a very determined man.

A friend of a friend with insider knowledge from the STV weather room told me there would be no thaw until after Boxing Day. It didn't seem possible but yet that's what happened. On one particularly cold day, I decided to check to see if the temperature really was minus 20 degrees and placed a thermometer on the back doorstep. It froze solid to the ice, which was all the information I needed.

Apart from struggling to go about our daily business, we were particularly worried that Matthew's class was due to go on a trip to the Christmas markets in Lille and Bruges. The school wouldn't cancel in case there was a thaw and the insurance company refused to pay out. In the meantime, a young girl was tragically killed when a coach taking her class on a school trip crashed and left the road, fuelling our fears even further. Days before the class trip was due to leave, it was finally cancelled.

Matthew was disappointed, of course, but Iain decided to make the most of the weather by holding a winter barbecue. We really should have put our foot down, but for some reason we let him go ahead and a rusty contraption that was to serve as the barbecue appeared in the garden. Iain and his friends then went off to buy the food, only to return with bags and bags of supplies from... Iceland (the frozen food store, not the country). Thrift had outweighed common sense, so I spent most of the afternoon cooking burgers, sausages, chicken thighs and more in the oven as they set up outside. And of course, the idea may have sounded exciting, but the reality was that not many of the 30 or so guests could cope with the cold, so we ended up with a full house that night as the abandoned barbecue burned outside.

Aside from serious health issues and freak weather conditions, I took on two additional challenges.

Since becoming a full member of ITI, I'd also joined its French and Media, Arts & Tourism (MAT) networks. The long-standing MAT coordinator had announced her intention to stand down but almost a year later, still nobody had stepped up to replace her. I'd considered putting myself forward but felt that I lived too far away from London, where the network events took place, to be able to run the network efficiently. When the coordinator said she would be going anyway and the network would fold, this ultimatum was the encouragement I needed to volunteer and I was duly appointed as her replacement. I'd taken on my first ITI volunteering role outside ScotNet.

The next challenge was in an area I'd been involved in since 2009, perhaps slightly earlier. Milngavie had a bookshop with a little café. After having coffee there one day with a friend, who happens to be a Spanish translator, we decided it would be a great place to hold a book group and enquired at the desk. It so happened that two sisters had also made the same suggestion, so we got in touch with them and together we founded the Milngavie Bookshop book group. It was also around this time that the owners of the bookshop and the art shop got together to hatch a plan to hold an annual book and arts festival in Milngavie. I immediately signed up as a volunteer for the

2009 inaugural festival. The next year, I joined the organising committee. It was extra work on top of my translations, but I loved every minute of it. It was great to take on a different role and offer creative or practical solutions to make the event a success.

At one of the committee meetings for the third festival in 2011, we applied for funding to pay for a project manager. What I didn't realise was that I was lined up for the job. The application was successful and I immediately received an email asking me to take on the role. I wasn't sure I'd have the time and energy to commit, so I agreed to go down to the bookshop to discuss the proposal. As I entered the shop all the staff members immediately congratulated me. It seems it was a fait accompli and I was to project-manage that year's festival in return for a flat payment of £2,000.

It was fun, exhausting, bonkers at times and such a learning curve.

I'd had experience hosting author events, but now I would need to organise them.

I'd met authors, but now I'd need to introduce some of them to the audience.

I'd helped the stallholders set up and run their stalls, but now I'd need to make sure they signed up for the 2012 festival and sort out the paperwork.

I'd helped the street entertainers with practical issues, but now I'd need to actually recruit them and make sure they turned up.

I'd helped out as a volunteer, but now I'd need to recruit and coordinate the volunteers.

I'd helped set up the halls, but now I'd need to make the bookings and all the arrangements.

I'd helped with ticket sales and social media posts, but now I'd need to actively seek publicity for the festival…

… and the list goes on.

Actually, I did particularly well on the publicity front. Not only did the local paper publish regular festival updates, and there was an article about it in Glasgow's Evening Times, but Malcolm also came back from the shops one Saturday waving his copy of the *i* newspaper. We'd made it into the national press.

We did have some big names to pull in the crowds. Julia Donaldson brought her stage show to the 2011 event, which attracted families from a much wider radius. The bookshop owner's niece was to appear in the show but ten minutes before the event she was nowhere to be seen. Julia asked if I would step in and handed me the bunch of flowers she was holding and started to instruct me about what I needed to do. And that, dear reader, is how I nearly ended up on stage in a

Julia Donaldson production… until the real 'actress' turned up with minutes to spare.

In addition to the main book events, we'd organised street entertainers, musicians and other fringe events for the Saturday. The headline act was a Beatles tribute band: Them Beatles. Christopher Brookmyre and Mark Billingham were to close the festival with what had become its famous Fish & Chips & Champagne Crime Night.

Of course, you can plan everything down to the very last detail, but that doesn't mean things won't go wrong. In previous years we'd had authors cancelling at the very last minute, hiccups with hall bookings and more, so I was ready to troubleshoot. I wasn't, however, prepared for the frenzy of the day and how much I'd have to coordinate.

A local bar always supplied the wine for the crime night, but this time it delivered perry instead. We'd previously blurred the 'champagne' boundaries by serving sparkling wine, but there was no way perry was a suitable substitute and it was too late for them to provide an alternative. Early afternoon I found myself reuniting two stray hip hop dancers with their troupe before doing a trolley dash round Tesco in a high-vis vest, buying enough sparkling wine for the evening and then checking that our main music act – Them Beatles – had arrived and were ready to go on stage. Before I knew it, I was in the hall for the evening event, popping corks and hoping that the fish suppers would turn up on time. I fell into bed that night and slept soundly.

The Saturday also happened to be the 50th birthday of Angela, my flatmate from London, who'd since moved to Edinburgh. I was disappointed that I couldn't go to her party, but her husband had organised a lunch for her and some friends in an Edinburgh restaurant the next day. Knowing that I'd be exhausted after the festival, I accepted her invitation to stay over and then booked a room in a posh hotel for the Monday night. I'd even booked a massage treatment for the Tuesday to relieve my aching legs. It was to be the perfect way to wind down from weeks of hard work, but it didn't exactly go to plan.

I was still in a complete daze as I got on the train the next morning. When I arrived at the restaurant for lunch, the waiter took my small suitcase to put in the cloakroom. Wine and food proved to be rather restorative, so the afternoon passed in a flash. However, alcohol and exhaustion are not a great mix and I managed to get back to A's house before I remembered my suitcase was still at the restaurant. Her extremely patient husband was sent back in a taxi to pick it up.

There was more food that evening and I took charge of my gluten-free rolls, burning myself on the AGA door in the process. Alcohol must have numbed the pain and it didn't look too bad, so I just put a plaster on it and continued to party.

I was dropped off at the hotel late afternoon on the Monday and had a leisurely meal and early night.

I woke feeling slightly more refreshed on the Tuesday morning and went down for breakfast. I noticed newspapers laid out on the reception desk but, because I was not a regular at posh hotels, I didn't know if they were complimentary and didn't want to ask. I decided I'd go to the Tesco a few doors down and buy my own. I entered the glass revolving door, my mind obviously still elsewhere, tried to exit too early and walked straight into a glass panel. I could literally see stars and feel a lump forming on my forehead, but, so as not to make a fuss, I continued on my way and bought the newspaper.

When I arrived back at the hotel, I discreetly asked a barman for some ice in a napkin and spent the hour before my treatment lying on my bed trying to reduce the swelling of the golf-ball-sized lump.

Unsurprisingly, Malcolm was rather concerned to see the state of me when I got back home that afternoon. The burn turned out to be more serious too, needing treatment at our local medical practice. So, when I say 'I once project-managed a book and arts festival and it nearly killed me', I mean literally as well as metaphorically. All in all, it had been a great experience, but I realised that I couldn't realistically repeat it the following year. A smaller-scale festival did take place in 2012, but it was to be the last and sadly both the bookshop and art shop closed a few years later.

Chapter 18

PRICE PRESSURE AND POETRY

It was probably early 2012 that I started receiving a lot of emails from my main agency client, except they weren't addressed to me personally, but sent to multiple recipients. At the time, I was working mainly for other branches of the company and almost exclusively on creative projects, but I couldn't help but notice that the rates offered in the bulk emails were considerably lower than mine and the deadlines were much tighter. Plus, if several people were receiving the same offer, it was logical that you'd need to be quick off the mark to answer first and secure the job. Although I wasn't directly affected at that time, it set alarm bells ringing. How long before I was asked to lower my rate or deliver to a really tight deadline? Worse still, what if the jobs I was currently guaranteed were farmed out using this system? It was obvious I'd need to prepare ahead in case this happened.

The first thing I decided to do was to get a website. Luckily, a friend from the book group, Jenny, happened to design websites, so she agreed to create a simple one for me. Because I'd worked almost exclusively on creative projects and been the go-to person for that type of translation at a particular agency, I decided that my website would promote my services as a creative translator and my friend Jenny – a woman of many talents – designed me a logo. So, it wasn't exactly a case of 'fake it till you make it' because I did have experience, just not working with direct clients. And of course, I still had to take on more general texts in the background to keep the money coming in.

I also created business cards featuring my new logo. I asked a local printer to produce the final cards and he had some trouble getting the colour of the logo correct. When he delivered a second template that still wasn't right, I had to invite him in to show him my microwave, as it was the exact colour that I wanted. He was rather surprised that someone would buy a purple microwave, but the next template could finally go to print.

I felt ready to hit the ground running but sadly my private life took centre stage again. Gordon had been diagnosed with lung cancer in 2010 and since then he had never been in remission, although there had been a gap in his chemo. He now needed more treatment and I was taking him to the hospital every other second week for infusions and making sure he was coping in between appointments.

It was a particularly stressful time and I'd been having some sort of alternative therapy to help me deal with it (possibly reflexology – I seem to have tried them all). One day at the clinic, I saw a poster advertising a self-hypnosis workshop and persuaded a friend, who was having an equally difficult time, to come along with me. She was a true alternative therapy sceptic but agreed to join me on the Saturday afternoon in question when, after a talk about stress and how it affected us, the therapist announced, 'You might want to visit the bathroom before I hypnotise you'. So much for the 'self-hypnosis' in the advert.

We all dutifully formed a queue and my friend said, 'I'm just going to pretend'. Although not a sceptic myself, I had to agree that was probably the best course of action because I hadn't come along to be hypnotised. I'd come along to be taught how to help myself relax and had fully expected we'd be asked to pair off and take it in turns to swing a necklace in front of our partner's eyes in the vague hope that something happened. This was obviously not what the therapist had in mind and, as it transpired, opting out was not on the agenda.

Within minutes I found myself in the deepest, most relaxing state I've ever experienced. My nose was itchy, but I couldn't raise my hand to scratch it. When we were brought round, we discovered that what we thought had been minutes had actually been nearly half an hour. I couldn't believe the therapist had had the power to switch off my mind with his voice, although he did mention my continuous rapid eye movement.

I was ready to sign up for a course of treatment on the spot, but thankfully he wasn't taking bookings because, as I drove my friend home, I realised I felt like I was drink-driving. After I dropped her off, I continued on my journey, passing a people carrier driven by a woman who looked like she had a Hitler moustache. When I encountered a dead seagull on the road round the corner from my house, I could hear it screeching for help. The hypnotherapy had certainly messed with my brain. Rather than panic – this was not the first or last strange experience I'd had with alternative therapies – I poured myself a glass of red and felt better after a good night's sleep.

As time went on, Gordon started to really struggle with chemotherapy. Several sessions were cancelled because his immune system wasn't strong enough to cope. At the end of July 2012, I noticed a marked deterioration in his health and on Sunday 5 August I realised he needed medical treatment. Apart from his physical condition, there were other signs. Gordon was a keen sportsman and had been following the London 2012 Olympics closely. When I asked him what he thought of Team GB's performance the previous evening, what was to become known as Super Saturday, he'd barely registered the achievements. And when he didn't want to watch the tennis final that day, where Andy Murray beat Roger Federer to win Olympic gold, I knew things were bad. He was admitted to hospital and, despite reassurances from the medical staff, the family was called in on the morning of Friday 10 August and he died that evening.

Thankfully, Matthew was in Aberdeen at a scout camp and so we didn't have to decide whether, aged 15, he was old enough to come with us to say goodbye to his grandad. Telling him the news when I picked him up from the coach on the Saturday evening was, however, one of the hardest things I'd had to do.

Gordon had been very involved with the family on an almost daily basis, having moved to Milngavie in retirement and left his friends behind in Chester, so his loss hit us hard. The boys were particularly close to their grandad and his was the first death of a close family member they had experienced.

Iain, then 20, insisted he wanted to do a eulogy at the funeral. As Gordon had no church connections in Scotland, the funeral directors sent along a 'minister' to meet us and arrange the service. I'd had my reservations about her from a phone call the previous evening when she said, 'He was Welsh so he'll want such and such a hymn'. Our experience the following day was an unmitigated disaster. She arrived with a checklist and was only interested in filling in the blanks. She upset Iain, who swore at her and left the room. The final straw was her insistence that she would end the ceremony with 'His order books are closed now'. Her suggestion was based on the fact that Gordon had been an estimating engineer but to us it was totally ridiculous. He had also loved cricket all his life but she dismissed our suggestion of 'his last innings' with, 'No, I like mine better'.

We ushered her out and sat there, not knowing what to do. Iain immediately came down and apologised to us with the words, 'My grandad told me always to stick up for myself'. It had not been our finest moment as parents, but he was

147

absolutely right. She was awful and she wouldn't do. We then organised an alternative celebrant and had to go through the whole process again. She was perfect and so supportive of Iain, who did his grandad proud on the day. Now, I'm someone who's always happy to go with the flow but my son had taught me a valuable lesson: it's fine to accept situations that are not quite right if they're not important but when it matters, you need to speak out and get what you want.

In fact, I would later discover that Gordon had left his affairs in the hands of a lawyer, who really wasn't, to put it mildly, half as good as our own. I let him do the absolute minimum but then told him we'd make our own arrangements to sell the house. He was taken aback, but I knew it was the right thing to do. I'm not sure I'd have done that had it not been for the incident with the funeral celebrant.

I'd been supporting Gordon through his treatment, both physically with lifts to and from the hospital and mentally as he came to terms with the return of the disease. Inevitably, I was suffering from stress-related stomach issues and was undergoing reflexology at the time. The therapist recommended acupuncture. I really didn't like the idea of having all those little needles punched into me but, despite my misgivings, I booked some sessions.

As I'd anticipated, it was horrible. At each visit I dreaded the needles and, despite reports that it sent you into an amazing, relaxed state, I felt absolutely nothing. I was about to stop the sessions when, one Friday afternoon, I drifted off into a state somewhere between conscious and unconscious. I subsequently had a fabulous night's sleep and, for some reason, woke up the next day wanting to write poetry.

It was a Saturday morning and I'd usually be getting up to go food shopping, but I stayed in bed with a notepad and wrote poem after poem. When I finally dragged myself to the supermarket, I was jotting down lines as I filled my trolley. I wish I could remember the exact sequence of events but I can't and the therapist was, naturally, baffled too. The experience wasn't repeated and I subsequently admitted defeat. Acupuncture was expensive and had done nothing for my health, but it had unlocked some sort of rhyming capacity in my brain and I went on to launch a blog of translation-themed poems, Chatter and Verse.

If I'd understood how to use Google analytics, I'd have realised how popular the blog was and kept it going, but I gave up after a while. Sadly, I've had other blog ideas that all suffered the same fate. Blogging wasn't for me, but there was always Facebook, which was becoming the outlet for my stories as I started to venture further afield.

Chapter 19

CONFERENCES, COPYWRITING
AND COOPERATION

The place is Gatwick, the month is May
The Hilton Hotel is where we'll stay

The Hilton? What's the reason why?
It's this year's conference of the ITI

Masterclasses a choice of four
Technology, money, could you ask for more?

Working the room is the other choice
Helping translators to find their voice

Drinks and dinner round off the first day
Before the conference gets underway

Soap and drugs, workflow and planes
CPD, export, social media and games

A yoga session to help us unwind
Stretch our limbs and empty our mind

Professional photos taken on site
A chance to get our image just right

Line dancing, whose idea was that?
Yes please I'll have a sparkly hat

As Sunday dawns there's lots in store
Quality, patents, contracts and more

Keynote speakers entertain and inspire
Figureheads we all admire

A final break with cakes and tea
Then singing translators with *Stand by me*

At the summary session we take a seat
And soon realise we're in for a treat

A conference video has been prepared
And we're the first to see it aired

Next, it's feedback, all positive of course
All in one voice, if a little hoarse

We ate and drank and had some fun
And learnt to look after number one

With knowledge gained at every session
We've pulled together as a profession

Hailed a success by all attending
For the conference committee a happy ending

The first of my adventures was to the ITI
Conference in Gatwick in 2013 and the poem says
it all. It was a fabulous experience and an
opportunity to meet in person all those colleagues
I'd been communicating with on Twitter and
Facebook. And in case you're wondering, we

donned sparkly Stetsons to round off the gala dinner with a spot of line dancing.

On the Sunday evening, when the Glasgow contingent hit a very busy Gatwick airport for our flight home – and the French nationals gave us Brits a masterclass in queue jumping at security – I knew that this conference wouldn't be my last. For translators who, at the time anyway, spent their working life alone in front of computers, it was not only a welcome opportunity to socialise but also a great way to keep up with trends, learn new skills and listen to the experts.

Of course, a conference isn't cheap and, I'll be honest, it was probably thanks to Gordon's inheritance that I could afford to attend this ITI conference *and* stay in the conference hotel, which is definitely worth doing if you can. When your brain gets frazzled, as it inevitably will, you can escape to your room to rest and recharge before embarking on the remainder of the packed programme. For anyone used to working at home in a quiet office with no interruptions, a conference can be a real assault on the senses. And it's not just introverts who need to find time for a little peace and quiet. At my first few conferences, I attended one session in absolutely every slot, but, with experience, I've learnt that it's not only acceptable but also recommended to pace yourself and plan some downtime.

This was the first of many new experiences that punctuated 2013, as I worked hard to develop my specialism and diversify my client base. My new website was online and I was able to promote it on social media to ensure colleagues thought of me as the go-to-person for French to English creative translations. Plus, having met some of these colleagues in person, they felt confident to refer work to me. It was in fact in August 2013 that I was first contacted by Moira Bluer, who asked me if I'd like to take on the creative translations she received from clients and we've been working closely ever since. We would go on to co-translate two books entitled *La créativité liée au vélo – Biked-inspired creativity* 1 and 2 by fellow translator Pascal Mageren in 2015 and 2020. In addition to her subcontracting work to me, she has since become the trusty editor not only of my translations but of this book, too.

By now I was also being asked by agencies if I could do copywriting for clients. Although I find writing easy, I felt I wanted to explore this particular skill further and have my work revised by a professional, so I obtained a diploma from what is now The College of Media and Publishing.

Initially, I thought I'd diversify into copywriting, but this has never happened, for three reasons:

- the agencies asking me to take on copywriting tasks were marketing it alongside translation, both at silly prices, and were precisely the type of client I was trying to move away from,

- I was a very experienced translator but a newbie copywriter. If I wanted to be

153

taken seriously, I'd need to find a way to establish myself in the industry alongside experienced copywriters,

- I had enough translation work.

So, I decided to offer copywriting services to small direct clients in my specialist areas. This hasn't happened either but my website still has a copywriting page offering this service. I've been approached twice by companies looking for a wine writer, which is, of course, a completely different skill and I've had to turn them down. But it's costing me nothing to keep the page there and it will possibly be an area I promote further in the future.

The same agencies were also asking me if I had a CAT tool so I decided to invest in Trados Studio. I had previously used Trados and Wordfast at different times but had let both licences expire because I didn't like using the tools for creative texts. However, I was still doing some other types of translation, so I dug deep and bought the latest version of Trados Studio and paid for an expensive training course in London with the aim of making the tool work for me.

I never did achieve that goal. To date, this has been my one and only CPD mistake. Many courses and events I've attended have been of no direct benefit to me, but I've always learnt something or met somebody that has led to something else. But I just don't have a brain that works well with segmentation.

After all the work and CPD, it was time for a bit of relaxation and in August 2013, Malcolm and I went on our first ever week-long holiday on our own without the kids. Iain was old enough to stay behind alone (who knows what happened at the house that week) and Matthew was at scout camp, so we seized the opportunity and booked an apartment in Berlin.

We'd had the odd weekend away, of course, but that was always on a budget. Indeed, we once flew with Ryanair to Milan and back for less than the cost of their in-flight muffins. We'd also had some fantastic summer holidays visiting friends, but we'd never booked accommodation for a whole week and been tourists in a city.

Actually, we did the touristy things during the day but felt like residents in the evening, as our apartment was in a residential block in a street just off Potsdamer Platz. It looked out over student accommodation and an unusual ivy-covered building and there was a Lidl at the end of the road. We also ate and drank in the local bars and restaurants.

Now, Malcolm always liked to know absolutely everything about a city and there was a building across the road from the flat with a plaque on the door. I was able to tell him it was some sort of guild hall, but there was no further information. He also spent the whole time we were away stopping people to ask if they knew where David Bowie had recorded his album back in the 70s. Nobody knew.

The Saturday we arrived back home, Malcolm logged on to his trusty computer to discover that Bowie had – completely out of the blue – released a new single *Where are we now?* and the promotional video had been partly filmed in the very street where we'd spent our holiday, complete with a shot of the ivy-covered building. After further research, the 'mysterious' building he'd been badgering me about all week turned out to be the Hansa Tonstudio, where Bowie had recorded in the 70s. Had we done our homework before travelling, I believe we could even have visited the studios.

It was back to business after our break and in October that year I travelled to London for the second workshop I'd arranged for the ITI Media Arts & Tourism network. The first, in November 2012, had been on art translation and was held at the same venue, Imperial College London South Kensington Campus. The topic for the 2013 workshop was literary translation and, on this occasion, we had a speaker for the first hour and then three network members joined him on a panel to share their own experience. This became the standard format of MAT workshops and was almost as popular as the macarons that always accompanied the working lunch that followed.

In November that year I travelled to London again, this time to a meeting of all the ITI network and regional coordinators.

In the space of two years, my working life had changed completely. The days sitting at the computer translating in silence were now punctuated with trips further afield, some expenses-paid, others tax-deductible and all of them extremely good for my mental health.

As a people person, I missed the office banter of my days of permanent employment. I even missed the commute. I admit, my journey to and from work in London hadn't involved many absolutely packed tube trains and my drive between home and the Glasgow office had been along a quiet country road. Both were great opportunities to wind down from the day at work and prepare myself for the evening ahead. By contrast, the short distance from office to kitchen at 5 o'clock was brutal. I'd still be thinking about work as I was met with an onslaught of questions, the most predictable being 'What's for dinner?'

Thankfully, I had another conference lined up for 2014.

Chapter 20

BUSINESS AND PLEASURE AT BP14

A conference in Budapest, that sounds like fun,
Many on offer but this could be the one,
A conference a year is my ultimate goal,
Good for my business, even better for my soul.

Fast forward some months and it's fait accompli
I arrive at the hotel, two colleagues with me
The rain pours down, the thunder booms
'Mr Happy' on reception messes up our rooms

But all is soon forgotten as we head for the city,
And are taken to a café that's really rather pretty,
After a convivial evening, I know one hundred
percent
It's going to be memorable, money well spent

The morning dawns, the real work starts
The focus a profession so dear to our hearts
A job we love, our true vocation
Of course this has to be translation

A keynote speech with a panel debate
The market is changing, so what's our fate?
The overall consensus: we'll find our way
Good translators are here to stay

Feel and think like an expert, act like one too

Wise words from a colleague that certainly ring
true
Knowledge workers must all join the campaign
It's not our fingers, it's what we do with our brain

Specialise, stand out, offer something more
Know what you're good at, find an area you
adore
Working with others is a viable option
One presenter has a system ready for adoption

CPD, branding, Easling, transcreation
Tourism, medical, quality, collaboration
The programme is vast, the topics diverse,
Far too many to include in this little verse

And after the learning there's plenty of fun
Time to relax, the hard work is done
Networking galore, meeting friends new and old,
Business cards exchanged experiences told

A cruise on the Danube, the view is divine
Good food washed down with exquisite wine
Some translators dance, others entertain
We all welcome the chance to rest our brain

After a gala dinner some head to the baths
Others gather at the hotel for last night laughs
As wine bottles are emptied, our sad thoughts we
banish
Our new-found friends are not going to vanish

With social media we'll all stay in touch,
United in an experience we enjoyed so much
And as for the next one we're relying on one man

Conference organiser extraordinaire, Csaba Ban.

And so, off to Budapest I went, for a trip that was going to take me out of my comfort zone in so many ways. Before then, I'd mainly visited countries in Western Europe where, as a linguist, I was able to use the languages I do speak to catch the gist of what's happening or what's being said. I'd tried to learn some Hungarian before I went but gave up in lesson three when the topic was drunken men and smelly dogs, or something similar, and would be totally irrelevant (I hoped) for my forthcoming adventure in a country where I couldn't understand one word of the written or spoken language. Of course, I wasn't alone among my fellow translators who attended the conference.

I made the journey to Budapest with two other colleagues and we booked a car to take us to the conference hotel. The driver spoke English, but, as the hotel was not in the tourist area, the reception staff were not so proficient. There was a terrible mix-up on arrival, as two of us had arranged to share a twin room with other colleagues but had been allocated singles. When I finally arrived in a suitable room, I was taken right back to the 70s with brown and beige floral tiles in the bathroom and a beige toilet seat that was barely attached. I felt like I'd just booked into Fawlty Towers.

I'd agreed to share for two nights with a translator from Croatia who'd booked for the conference at the last minute when there were no more rooms available at the hotel. I'd never met her, but I reckoned that even if in the unlikely event it was a disaster, it wasn't for all four nights. Plus, it helped with the cost.

Of course, she was absolutely lovely and spoke great English. In fact, this was a conference being held in English, a language which, for the vast majority of attendees, was not their mother tongue. I was one of only a handful of native English speakers and the experience was truly humbling.

My roommate arrived late afternoon on the second day and neither of us had booked for the buffet that was being held later, so we headed into town. Having strict dietary requirements in a country where you don't speak the language was daunting, so we settled for TGI Fridays in the centre of Budapest. And what a contrast this was. The waiter spoke perfect English, the menu was in English and the customer service experience was second to none. At this point, when I was still feeling the culture shock, it was a haven of familiar in the midst of so many unknowns.

On the day after we arrived, a group of us went on an organised walking tour of the city, which ended at the castle, where the guide handed out bus tickets and pointed us in the direction of the bus stop. We were still disorientated in a city we barely knew and couldn't for the life of us find our way down to the bus stop. Nobody seemed to speak English and none of us spoke Hungarian.

When we finally did get to the bus stop it was out of service because the road was closed for May Day celebrations. We thought about a taxi, but we had no idea how much it would cost and – more to the point – not one of us could pronounce the name of the hotel. Thankfully, a colleague who had arrived a day earlier than most of us had already used the underground system so, when we hit upon a station, she was able to get us back to the hotel.

Of course, once the conference started and I met more and more lovely people, this all became a distant memory and I began to grow very fond of the hotel and its staff. As I arrived at breakfast each morning, the same waiter would run into the kitchen and appear with a brand-new loaf of gluten-free bread and an unopened carton of soya milk. At the first conference lunch, I was served a huge plate of salad. 'OK, I thought. Not very filling, but at least I know it's safe.' Then I was presented with an equally large plate of roasted vegetables. It so happened that many of my colleagues at the same table were vegetarian and for them the only option was spaghetti with a simple tomato sauce. They were only too happy to help me eat the veggies and were as surprised as I was when the empty plate was replaced by a chocolate cake made specially for me by the chef.

Without a doubt, the highlight of my trip was an evening dinner cruise on the Danube. We set off while it was still light and enjoyed a nice meal as we sailed up the river past the Hungarian parliament and other buildings. By the time the boat turned round it was dark, so the return journey was spent on the dancefloor as we took in Budapest by night. Some of us then followed a local translator to a bar in the old town for Margaritas.

But we were also in Budapest to work, and this was only the first in a series of BP conferences that have been superbly organised by Csaba Ban and his wife Zita. I'm still in touch with many of the people I met there (thank you, Facebook) and, apart from finding so many lovely new friends, there was an unexpected bonus. For once, French to English was not one of the predominant language combinations and I've since had a lot of work passed on by BP14 attendees who previously had little or no contact with a French to English translator.

I was definitely expanding my horizons and meeting colleagues from so many different countries, but I decided it was time to venture beyond the world of translation and attend events where I would meet my target clients.

Chapter 21

ALISON'S ADVENTURES IN CLIENTLAND

Of course I'll go, it's something new
And definitely time my business grew

The event is free so that's a plus
Networking? Don't understand the fuss

I'm no shrinking violet, or so I'm told
So what's the problem for one so bold?

New cards, nice suit and business head
I'm ready for action… what's that you said?

No, it's my first, of many I hope
It won't be easy but I'm sure I'll cope

Damn and blast it where's the map?
Not yet a panic, just a bit of a flap

OK I'm not early, but not that late
Just remember it's not a date

No-one is waiting just for you
But, oh my God, what do I do?

With a beating heart of increasing pace
I scan the room for a familiar face

I'm on my own, there's no other way

I'll just have to think of something to say

I approach a group deep in conversation
But stop in my tracks as the topic's inflation

Deciding I need some time to think
I head for the table to have a drink

I grab a water and down it in one
Desperately fighting the urge to run

Group number two looks a better bet
Just need to do it, no time to vet

'Do you mind if I join you?' I say to be nice
It does the trick and breaks the ice

'My name is Jan' one says with a smile
Is this your first event in a while?

'Yes,' I say, 'well, to tell the truth.
First event ever, shaky hand's the proof.'

'Only my second so I feel your pain.
But little to lose and lots to gain'

Her words of encouragement are all I need
I join the group and am soon up to speed

Explaining the work of a freelance translator
I discover a client who may need me later

Cards are exchanged, it's time to move on
And now I no longer feel so forlorn

It certainly wasn't as easy as expected
But a couple more and I could have this
perfected.

Does this sound familiar? How many events have you gone to where you've not known anybody else and had to find a way to break the ice and join a conversation? In fact, this poem was based on advice I was once given. Rather than simply sidling up to a group of people and hoping they'll include you, why not say 'Do you mind if I join you?'?

I put this networking tip into practice several times as I started to go to client events. It's one thing attending a gathering of people you've met before or have at least interacted with previously on social media or another platform; it's quite another landing somewhere among industry experts who most probably already know each other well. You're the outsider in this case and have to find a way to join a conversation and sound both knowledgeable and eager to learn more.

In actual fact, because I advertise myself as a French to English translator for the creative industries, I often find myself working in a wide range of areas, including jewellery, fashion, cosmetics, food and drink, and the Arts. I also capitalise on the years I spent in the wines and spirits industry and my Wine and Spirits Education Trust (WSET) level 2 qualification to promote French wine and champagne as a niche specialism.

So 'industry' can be a very broad term for me, but the first non-translator event I attended was fashion-related and the opportunity came about thanks to the generosity of a Dutch colleague, Percy Balemans, who is well known for specialising in this area. She happened to mention on Facebook that she was going to a small conference being run by the Institute for Fashion Heritage in Arnhem on 20 June 2014, and I expressed an interest. She immediately offered to put me up for a few days and take me with her.

Not long afterwards, I landed at Amsterdam airport and made my way to her small village by train, ready for what was to be my first venture into the world of fashion. It was a small affair, and the official working language was English, so less daunting. Plus, we had each other for moral support, and I was wearing a pair of amazing shoes with fuchsia mirror heels that I'd bought in Marks & Spencer's sale for £15. When a fellow attendee admired them, I completely missed the opportunity to say 'Prada, darling' and I'm not terribly sure she was impressed to hear about my M&S bargain. As an aside, this was to be the one and only outing for these shoes because they were totally impractical.

In the afternoon we decided to attend separate sessions. I was in a group of about 15 led by the fashion illustrator, and former editor of the Dutch edition of Harper's Bazaar, Piet Paris. He assumed we were all Dutch speakers and launched into his session in his native language. I could either sit quietly or make myself known. I plucked up courage and raised my hand to ask him to speak English just for me.

My second adventure was a solo one. The Culture Action Europe conference in Newcastle in October 2014 appeared on my Twitter timeline and was relatively inexpensive. I was tempted but also scared witless, so I didn't book right away. But it preyed on my mind. Maybe if I checked travel and hotel costs it would prove to be prohibitive? No such luck, so I bit the bullet and signed myself up.

I arrived the day before just in time for an evening talk, which I attended alone. On the day of the conference, I chatted to a few more people, as it's so much easier to strike up a conversation with someone you're sitting beside than to approach a group of people when they're standing around talking.

In the afternoon we were split into groups of eight to critique a paper in an area I knew absolutely nothing about. I really did feel like an outsider, especially when I introduced myself as a translator and was met with nothing short of astonishment. Thankfully, I'd rehearsed in advance what I was going to say, which went something like this:

I'm here to learn about the industry and how you speak. I also want to reassure you that, despite advances in machine translation, translators have not disappeared. You need us. You need our brains to understand nuances. So we're here to stay.

Of course, I paraphrased the above so as not to reinforce my 'outsider' status and sound like a robot, but it led to an interesting conversation at tea break when a fellow group member told me she'd no idea there was such a thing as a translation industry.

It also led to the group calling upon my translator/writer brain to help them phrase some of the amendments they were proposing to the paper that was in the process of being ripped to shreds (metaphorically) by everyone present. When the time came for the groups to present their findings at the plenary session, there were only two of our group remaining, as the others had left early to catch transport home. There was nothing for it but to join the other girl at the front and smile when she mentioned they'd been extremely fortunate to have a translator in their midst to help with the grammar and wording. And this translator had also been fortunate to learn a significant amount about smart cities, a topic I have since translated about on several occasions.

Feeling very pleased with myself, I headed to the station, only to find my ticket rejected at the barrier. It was Friday rush hour, so I had to step aside and look for someone to help. When I did eventually find a member of staff, the mystery was quickly solved. I'd booked my return journey for the same date in November, not October. I was a month early! My only option was to dig deep and pay £50 for a single ticket to Glasgow and promise myself I'd be more careful in future when making online bookings (and maybe do it <u>before</u> the first glass of red on a Friday night!).

These were smallish events but great confidence boosters. The once painfully shy schoolgirl who had still felt intimidated at the start of her very first ITI conference was out in the big bad world engaging with potential clients.

Chapter 22

PLAYING MY CARDS RIGHT

I click on 'send' the job is done
Delighted with the new client I've won

A bite to eat, now time to wind down
At a yoga session in the town

Some me-time I'm definitely taking
I need a stretch, my limbs are aching

Changed, mat in hand, I head to the car
But alas I don't get far

The ringing phone not yet on silent
Displays the number of my new client

Extra files, what did he mean?
Were there files I hadn't seen?

How on earth did this occur?
The week's been long, the start a blur.

'No, no, these files I wrote this morning,
I do apologise for the lack of warning

I'm afraid they're urgent, is that OK?
I hoped to have them by end of day'

Of course I'll do them right away,

Well, what else was there to say?

These days, I actually rarely come across the scenario in this poem, which was written back in 2013. It was more common when I was working exclusively with agencies and, in these situations, you normally have to take the project manager's word for it that the task is urgent. But in late 2014 I started to find more work in my specialist areas. My networking was definitely paying off and I was gaining some direct clients.

Much as I was delighted with my progress, I did find working with direct clients a very different proposition to working with agencies. If an agency is doing its job properly, the bulk of the responsibility is taken out of your hands, as is a percentage of the fee of course. The first few times an enquiry arrived in my inbox out of the blue, I felt a mix of excitement and trepidation. As most prospective clients wrote to me in French, my annual visits to France to keep up my fluency in the language came into their own. But that was only half the battle. I had to give a price and deadline and it took me a long time to adapt. Naturally, I'd quote higher than my agency rate but I didn't realise initially that the companies I was dealing with had higher budgets and weren't operating to the ridiculously short timescales that agencies expected. I've since learnt from experience that if a client says a request is urgent, they might be expecting 1,500 words to be returned the same week, not the same day.

Most of my new clients were (and still are) referred to me by colleagues or posted in a translator Facebook group or on an ITI network egroup.

For example, one morning a colleague posted a request on the ITI French Network group for someone to translate a rap poem for a Belgian magazine. The idea immediately appealed, but, as this was before the fortuitous acupuncture appointment, I had no idea if I could do it. I contacted him anyway and said I'd no other work on that morning, so, if nobody else had replied, I'd be happy to spend an hour (unpaid) experimenting with it to see what happened. He agreed and I found that after the first five minutes I was in the zone. I went on to do the job for a generous rate and the client was delighted with the translation. This particular colleague sent me fairly regular work from his client afterwards as a result.

Another opportunity came through a French translator whose website I'd translated into English. She contacted me a few months later to say that she volunteered for a Franco-Indian film festival and they were looking for someone to translate some documents pro bono from French to English. Did I know anyone?

As pro bono work can be a taboo subject, I was unsure about passing on the job or even mentioning it to colleagues, so I took a look at what it involved. It was around 2,500 words, so not excessive, and actually pretty high profile. The films were being shown at the Gaumont Champs Elysees and the event was sponsored by Paris city council. Could this be an opportunity for me to make connections?

This may well have been the case because I was invited to attend the event. I even received an email asking me what time I'd like a car to pick me up from my hotel. However, 'life happened' and it clashed with a family occasion that was too important to miss. More about that in chapter 24…

And some new clients have come from completely out of the blue. Remember my father-in-law's lawyer? A few months after Gordon died, I received a letter from him in the post. Oh dear, had he undercharged us? Were there still some loose ends to tie up? No, he had a client with business to sort out in France and wondered if I could translate the documents. How did he know I was a French to English translator? When he asked for my phone number, I left my business card.

After all, a certain Mr Snozzi had once left behind his card in a hotel restaurant and look where that led. Admittedly, he'd probably not been expecting a letter from an unemployed graduate a year later looking for a job, never mind the same graduate turning up in his office having arrived in France with nowhere to live.

This scenario was very different but the outcome equally unexpected and beneficial, for me anyway. Handing out business cards at a translation conference had always seemed pretty pointless to me, especially since you'll be taking home a list of attendees and most people are contactable through social media or a directory nowadays. I had to find something useful to do with my pretty purple cards, so I started to hand them out every time someone asked for my phone number. The vast majority probably ended up in a desk drawer, at best, or even the bin, but you never know who might need your services one day or where your card may end up.

Without wanting to jinx my dealings with direct clients, I can safely say I've yet to come across a really difficult one. Some have been rather odd, some of the translations have been really tricky and sometimes payments haven't arrived on time, but a diplomatic email has always done the trick. And others have been absolutely delightful, like the one in Paris, who took me to lunch when I was visiting the city. If it weren't for client confidentiality obligations, I could tell you some stories about the more eccentric ones but mum's the word.

So, as we neared the end of 2014, I was in a much happier place and a more secure position. I'd expanded my client base considerably, had amazing experiences away from my desk and met some great people along the way. Plus, I was being paid more than the paltry rate my previous agency clients were now offering so was able to spend less time at my desk on a day-to-day basis. More time for yoga… without any unfortunate interruptions.

Chapter 23

NOW I'M TALKING…

Agency, agency go away,
Don't come back till you've more to pay.
A brave step for me as no work I've got
But in a downward spiral I've been caught.

There was a time, not long ago,
When my agency rates were not so low.
But downward pressure is what they say,
And tell you your rate they just can't pay.

There's no way out, or so I believe
But it's a great profession, I don't want to leave.
So what is next, what do I do now?
I need to move forward but I don't know how.

Social media? The box is ticked
My specialist subjects I have picked
It's all so hard, I moan and groan
To move myself out of my comfort zone.

Self-promotion that's not my style,
I'll mull it over for a while.
But two hours later it's crystal clear,
What's holding me back is just plain fear.

That's it, time to take myself in hand,
If better clients I want to land...

This was the position I'd found myself in and had overcome, so when the call for papers for the 2015 ITI Conference in Newcastle was issued, I wondered whether sharing that experience might be useful to others.

In fact, I often noticed that attendees – especially at more local translation events – would find talks on marketing or networking extremely interesting but the ideas too daunting or expensive. Perhaps they had a young family so couldn't go away for more than one night? They might be the sole breadwinner so couldn't afford to invest in high-profile client events. Some had a steady income flow so were, understandably, happy to continue with no thought for the future. It all seemed beyond their reach, so they did absolutely nothing…

In my case, I'd been well and truly caught out, but when I found myself having to act pretty damn quick in response to the changing market conditions, I realised that I'd actually been doing quite a lot with limited time and resources. I was the sole breadwinner with a young family, so I couldn't afford to spend a fortune on really big events outside the translation industry. I'd done what was within my reach and was actually in a pretty good place to move forward.

On this basis, I submitted a proposal for the conference entitled 'It's not what you spend but the way that you spend it'. The idea was to share how I had marketed my services, undergone CPD and raised my profile within the industry on a very low budget. The proposal wasn't accepted right away but put on the reserve list. I did, I confess, breathe a sigh of relief. Maybe actually presenting was a step too far? The topic was obviously not going to be popular. I could now go to the conference as an attendee and enjoy the event. I came up with every excuse in the book to convince myself that submitting a proposal had been a bad idea, and then… one evening a few weeks later I received an email to say another presenter had cancelled. I was top of the reserve list. Would I still be willing to give my presentation?

My initial reaction was panic! However, my lovely colleague Anne de Freyman reassured me I'd have plenty of support, so I agreed. I would now actually have to commit my ideas to paper and create a PowerPoint presentation that was fit for an association of the ITI's standing.

As it happened, the PowerPoint was the easy bit. I arranged my thoughts into a series of bullet points in what was a very basic presentation. However, no matter how hard I tried, I couldn't write down everything I planned to say. I just couldn't get it out of my head and into a document. In fact, I never did manage to commit it to words. After one last failed attempt to put pen to paper on my train journey to the conference, I decided it was my story, so I'd manage by following the bullet points on the slides… and then crossed my fingers that I wasn't setting myself up for a massive failure.

In the meantime, the conference programme had been issued. There would be parallel sessions in three rooms of different sizes: the main hall where the plenary sessions were held, a medium-sized room and a small room that seated around 45 people. I'd been allocated the smallest of the three and the final session of the conference. On the plus side, my debut session would inevitably be small and some delegates would have left by then. On the minus side, I had the whole conference to stress about it.

And stress I did, because everyone I talked to told me they were coming to my session. I rehearsed the presentation once or twice in my bedroom and decided I could do nothing more. I should go and enjoy the conference, which I did but not quite as much as others where I'd had no active part to play in the event.

The break before my session arrived and I went to the room to set up, only to find a queue already forming. When the doors were opened there was what seemed like a deluge, with people sitting on the floor and standing at the back. This in itself was odd because there had been strict number control at other sessions, so I decided the organising committee had just let it go since we were nearing the end of the conference.

I began rather shakily but soon got into the flow and felt it had gone very well. As people were leaving, a colleague appeared from nowhere and asked me if I was aware of what had been happening while my session was in progress. I looked at him blankly. Quite apart from anything else, my mind was fully focussed on the slides lest I slip up and prove my lack of proper preparation had been presumptuous folly.

It transpires that a further 40 or so people had been turned away and gone into another session, only to be told that I was being moved into the medium-sized room. So they all arrived back downstairs. But it was too late to swap rooms, as both sessions had already started. As conference speaking goes, I'd actually had a pretty spectacular debut and I was subsequently asked to give my talk to other ITI networks.

So what was it all about? Simply everything I've written about so far. How I'd managed to move away from the lower end of the market with limited resources. But before I moved on to money-saving tips, I began with a list of expenses I consider non-negotiable:

- membership of a professional organisation, because my ITI membership had enhanced my status and brought me work through the directory and referrals,
- professional indemnity insurance, because I felt this gave potential clients confidence in me as a professional,
- an accountant, because mine had saved me work and ensured I didn't miss out on anything I was entitled to,
- business cards, because anything can happen when you leave your card behind,

- a website and domain name, another mark of professionalism,
- at least one conference a year, for the experience, the travel and work opportunities from colleague referrals,
- expenditure on my health, because, as I misquoted Maya Angelou 'Nothing will work unless you do',
- and an annual visit to France to keep up my spoken French.

I'm a firm believer in spending money on things that matter then finding inventive ways to do CPD and market my services with little or no budget. In this part of my talk, I spoke about volunteering to organise events because then you get to attend for free, looking for free events locally or paying for inexpensive webinars, subscribing to industry magazines and using social media.

I talked about the importance of having a specialism, as bottom-end agencies were cutting rates and post-editing of machine translation was looming on the horizon. And how you could develop this specialism through free courses or perhaps obtain funding from local organisations (Skills Development Scotland in my case).

You could even share your knowledge by talking at a conference, I suggested, as the conference fee is usually waived for speakers. In retrospect, this was probably pretty pretentious coming from a first-time speaker, but that speaking opportunity subsequently opened many doors for me.

I shared some stories and finished with a final message:

- engage, engage, engage (speak to people wherever you are),
- grow your confidence (maybe one day you will go to that high-profile industry event?),
- think ahead (and don't get caught out),
- keep your business head on at all times,
- take small steps (they're less daunting, but they all add up).

Was I sharing a success story? It depends on how you define success. In terms of income, I was working less and earning more, but I certainly wasn't in the high-income bracket.

In terms of work/life balance, mine had definitely improved.

In terms of enjoying life, I was having a blast.

And did I subsequently up my game and move into the premium market? Well, it depends how you define 'premium' but perhaps I didn't move forward as much I would have liked because– as you're about to find out – life happened!

Chapter 24

DRIVING [AND] EXPECTATONS

For context, I need to go back to the summer of 2014 when Glasgow hosted the Commonwealth Games. There was a great buzz in the city and my sister and I had been given two sets of four tickets for the athletics by my cousin and her husband, who were no longer able to use them. We had a spare ticket because Iain was in Paris and London with his girlfriend, Lauren, so we invited Malcolm's cousin, Debbie, to join us. I've never been a sports fan and Malcolm hated The Proclaimers, but the home team did really well and such was the atmosphere in the stadium that we were both belting out the Proclaimers' hit *I would walk 500 miles* with the crowd by the end of the night.

Iain and Lauren arrived back on the Sunday morning and Debbie was due to leave that evening. After a lovely day in Glasgow with Debbie, we were sitting in the living room before I took her to the station and Iain joined us. He very rarely left his loft bedroom when he was home, so I assumed he'd made a special effort to come and meet Debbie. He chatted about their week away, but, call it mother's instinct, I felt there was something that hadn't quite gone to plan. They hadn't done everything on their list because Lauren was tired. 'Fair enough,' I thought. 'They both lead busy lives'.

When he was still sitting in the living room after I got back from dropping Debbie at the station, I knew he wanted to tell me something. Before I'd even sat down, he said:

'Mum, you know how you always said you wanted grandchildren?'

I knew what was coming but was too busy trying to remember when I'd said I'd wanted grandchildren that I didn't react right away.

'Well, Lauren's pregnant. You're going to be a granny,' he blurted out.

Becoming a granny might not have been on my list of priorities at that time, but there are decisions in life that are not yours to take and, truth be told, I was delighted. He told his dad and then Matthew and, for the first time in ages, we found ourselves all gathered in the living room as he phoned his gran (who had definitely been dropping big hints that she wanted great-grandchildren).

The months that followed were a blur of ups and downs as they hit hurdles and medical scares (Lauren's back went out) and tried to decide where they were going to live. There were wonderful moments too, like when I discovered that, after being surrounded by men for much of my adult life, we were going to have a granddaughter. They invited Lauren's mum and me to a 3D scan near the end of the pregnancy and the baby stubbornly refused to move (now she's seven years old and I can see this is one of the character traits she developed early).

At this point, Lauren was back home living with her parents in Kilbirnie, a small town in Ayrshire, and they decided this is where they would live. They finally found a house to rent just three weeks before Grace Isabella arrived on 2 April 2015.

She was beautiful (of course) and still is, but Malcolm and I suddenly found ourselves bumped up a generation and about to embark on a whole new experience. The first time you babysit a grandchild and realise you're in charge of your own offspring's pride and joy is daunting, to say the least.

And what was even more daunting was the 30 miles and, crucially, motorway between us. Having worked from home for the past 18 years I'd managed to avoid motorway driving and wasn't at all keen to start again. However, needs must and the first drive to Kilbirnie was the nightmare I expected. I hesitated at junctions, got stuck in the wrong lane on a busy three-lane section very close to the exit I needed to take, and even hit upon (but thankfully didn't actually hit) an equally inept driver. I could see her approaching in the inside lane as I was about to merge. She didn't move lanes and arrived at the slipway just as we did. I had no option but to stop. And what did she do? She stopped and waved me out. Now, I may have done something wrong too, but I'm pretty sure stopping in the inside lane to let someone onto the motorway is a cardinal sin. However, my trembling 'backseat driver' in the passenger seat (Malcolm) blamed me.

I'd love to say I got more relaxed with the journey over time but that would be a lie. I didn't have any more surreal incidents but each time found myself sitting rigid on the sofa holding my granddaughter. And the worst thing was that, for as long as they lived in Kilbirnie (and didn't drive), I had no option but to do the drive… until one day, when Grace was about eight months old, I noticed a sign to Largs at the end of their road.

'Is Kilbirnie near Largs?' I asked Lauren.

'It's only 15 minutes down that road,' she replied.

I'd not been to Largs before, but I knew it was beside the sea, so on our next visit we drove down to take a look. The sun was shining that day as we ate chips on a bench looking out over the water to the island of Cumbrae.

'We could live here,' I said to a startled Malcom. Now, he was used to my hairbrained schemes and usually came round to the idea that yes, we did need a new bathroom or yes, we did need to extend the kitchen, but normally not until all the work had been done. He preferred the status quo at home, so this was likely a step too far.

However, I persuaded him that, as Matthew had moved into a student flat with friends, we didn't need to stay in Milngavie for his university commute (it would definitely have been more problematic, but not impossible, from Largs). Plus, Iain and Lauren had asked us to look after Grace one day a week once Lauren went back to work and, going by the rate Malcolm and I were arguing about my driving, his nerves, and the awful journey, we'd be divorced within a year if we had to do it weekly. He agreed and, by the time Grace was christened the following February, we were ready to house-hunt – or rather flat-hunt – in Largs. My criteria were, in fact, quite specific: a flat with a balcony and a sea view. Note the use of the first person. As I'd been the one who did the housework and gardening, I decided I had the prerogative and Malcolm agreed.

We booked a local hotel for Grace's christening and the next morning set off to view a few properties. The first was a flat in town, which was small and uninspiring. If I'm honest, it was too much like a retirement flat and, having become grandparents, we were already feeling ancient. That was an immediate 'no'. Next, we viewed a tiny house with a garden that backed onto the local Kwik Fit tyre specialist. I don't think I need to spell out why we didn't take that one further. The final property we'd arranged to see that day was a second-floor flat halfway between the town and the yacht haven. In fact, we very nearly didn't make the appointment, because it was an ugly 1970s building, but we decided it was worth a viewing since we were in Largs anyway. As we climbed the two flights of stairs, we were each independently deciding that, without a lift, it wasn't a sensible choice in our late 50s. The flat itself was a marked improvement on the other properties and, with patio doors and a glass balcony facing the Island of Cumbrae, very nearly had the sea view. It was bright and spacious but still not quite right.

The next time I came down to view a flat, it was a solo trip, as Malcom wasn't big on house-hunting and had actually not seen our second house in Milngavie until the day we got the keys. The flat in question was in a building I had a hunch we'd end up living in (so much for intuition). I'd also noticed on the website the previous day that there was another flat for sale in the block next to the third property we'd viewed previously. Tempted by the £25,000 cheaper asking price, I ignored the fact it was on the third floor and huffed and puffed up the stairs behind the estate agent, convinced I would dismiss it immediately. But the minute I stepped into the living room with the vast windows and glass fronted balcony overlooking the water I was sold. I arranged a second visit with a friend and the following Monday we made an offer. However, unbeknownst to us, the laws had changed in Scotland and we couldn't secure the property until we had funding in place, and that meant we needed to have a firm offer on our own house.

It was all systems go and a bit of a blur if I'm honest. I do remember taking a phone call from the lawyer in my hotel room in Prague, where I was attending BP16. The second people to view our house had made a very good offer. Would I agree to a six-week entry date? As that was the norm back when every offer in Scotland was a firm one – and I was getting ready to go out on the town with fellow conference attendees – I agreed.

Of course, this offer was not firm, as the purchasers still had to arrange their mortgage. We expressed interest in the Largs flat but had to wait until we had a firm offer on our house before we could confirm our own. Luckily, the Milngavie property market was fast moving and the turnover of property in Largs was (at the time) much slower. It was a tense few weeks.

Finally, a week before the agreed entry date, we were in a position to make a firm offer on the flat but then discovered that our 86-year-old vendor had gone away for the weekend and couldn't be contacted. We wouldn't get an answer until she got back home. We busied ourselves packing boxes and getting rid of years of junk – because who doesn't accumulate things when they have plenty of cupboards? – until we finally had our offer accepted on the Monday morning.

Our relief and delight were short-lived when we realised that we had to move four days later and we hadn't booked a removal company. The local ones were busy, but one put us in touch with a company nearer to Largs and thankfully they were available on the Friday. Finally, the gods were with us… until our vendor's solicitor went AWOL the day before the move. The Glasgow office thought he was in the Ayr office, and vice versa. And his phone was switched off. We never did find out where he had been – and, to be honest, it was the least of our worries at the time – but I suspect he might have found himself in a little bother after that escapade.

Anyway, to get back to the story, we found ourselves gathered in the lounge one last time (Iain had come back to say a final farewell to his family home), eating a takeaway, with absolutely no idea if we would get the keys to the flat the next day. I'd had to phone the removal company to explain the situation and they were amazing. Normally, if house contents are going into storage, they'd send a van with a container, but, as we didn't know whether or not they were, they agreed that – in the worst-case scenario – they'd take the loaded van back to their warehouse for the weekend and deliver on the Monday, at no extra cost.

So, on the Friday morning they left Milngavie with a full van, heading for Largs unless they heard otherwise. I finally got the call to collect the keys at 1pm and we packed the remainder of our possessions into the car and set off to our new home. I felt so sorry for the removal men, especially the one who ended up flat on his back with my (empty) filing cabinet on top of him near the end of the lengthy unloading operation, but they were troopers and had certainly saved the day.

So, on 27 May 2016, a mere three months after taking steps to make it happen, we sat down among the boxes in our new flat on the beautiful west coast of Scotland. We'd done it and a whole new adventure awaited us.

Chapter 25

CATCHING THE COACH [BUG]

In retrospect, we'd moved without doing too much research about Largs. I suspected there might be a coffee shop, a couple of pubs and perhaps a restaurant or two. On my first proper walk through the town, I counted over 30 places to eat and/or drink, including the famous Nardini's Art Deco restaurant and ice cream parlour. We would soon be sampling some of their delights when it became obvious our upgrade work on the flat would have to happen sooner rather than later.

It took less than 24 hours to discover that neither the cooker nor fridge freezer were fit for purpose. We also had to install central heating and opted to use a local company that could do it all. In the meantime, I decided to buy a mini-fridge and – purely by mistake (!!!) – bought a wine fridge. It was absolutely hopeless for storing chilled staples in a heatwave (well, a Scottish heatwave) but still sits in my office and comes into its own every Christmas.

Before the work could begin, we had to bring mains gas into the flat. When you've never before had to consider the infrastructure of a building, in this case a block of flats, this is far from easy and led to us breaking the communal rules within four weeks of arriving. I was in Glasgow the day the

191

gas installers arrived, and Malcolm and Matthew had a visit from a neighbour who was concerned about the position of the meter and boiler. Neither of them understood what he was talking about so decided to ignore it and didn't even bother mentioning it to me on my return. It wasn't until we were coming back home from town on the day the boiler was installed, and I saw a black pipe protruding from the front of the building – in a block where all protrusions and pipes had to be at the rear – that they happened to mention the neighbour's visit. I felt sick. Thankfully, our neighbours were understanding, although I'm not sure they believed my genuine plea that I had no idea that a boiler needed this pipe thing (flue) sticking out of the wall. The rules have since been relaxed.

The move to a flat was a downsize, which, in addition to releasing money for the upgrade, allowed me to take a few weeks off work until the upheaval was over and – most importantly of all – we finally had a broadband connection. I've never been able to work with noise and distraction, so this was reassuring, and my understanding clients were happy to wait for their translations or pass them on to colleagues I recommended.

On the other hand, the move propelled us one step further into the next stage of our lives. We seemed to be doing all this 'old age' stuff far too early. And my pre-granny bucket list had gone completely out of the window! So, it was only natural that the next step would be a coach tour.

Actually, our trip to Spain was far from a pensioners' outing. I noticed an advert for Riviera holidays in the newspaper one Saturday and immediately felt it would solve our holiday dilemma. Anywhere we went, Malcolm had to be constantly on the go and off exploring and never understood why sometimes I just wanted to sit and unwind with a book. I decided that this was the perfect solution, my logic being that while we were travelling between places, I could relax and he would have the impression that he was actually doing something. But we were still unsure about the organised holiday aspect. Then one day on Facebook a friend mentioned she was travelling through Andalusia and I asked her about the region, mentioning the tour we had in mind. By complete coincidence, one of her Facebook friends was a tour guide with Riviera Travel. She assured me that their tours weren't a military operation and that we'd also have time for ourselves, so we took the plunge and booked a Classical Spain trip for October 2016.

We chose October to avoid the extreme heat the region is famous for, but, as we monitored the temperatures in the week before departure, we saw them reaching 30 degrees Celsius and more. The region was having an unseasonal heatwave and there was nothing we could do about it, or so we thought – until fate intervened.

Unfortunately, our saving grace was Matthew severing tendons while chopping a carrot (note to parents who are preparing their kids for leaving home: don't buy them a set of brand-new knives if

193

yours at home couldn't cut butter). On the Thursday night he phoned from the hospital to tell me what had happened and that he was having surgery the next day. By now it was 9.30pm and his flatmates had sorted out what had been, by all accounts, a bit of a blood bath. They had taken him to the small injuries' clinic by taxi and, when they discovered it wasn't such a small injury, had gone with him in the ambulance to the hospital. It wasn't a blue-light ride; it was just those heady pre-Covid days when ambulances were available to do non-urgent transfers.

We immediately knew that we couldn't fly off to Spain on the Saturday and leave him, so we were refunded through insurance and booked again for the following April. Again we chose a month that should avoid the extreme heat (average temperatures were reported to be mid-20s); again the temperatures rose to over 30. Thank heavens for air-conditioning, which was so extreme in one hotel that we had to put on jumpers while in our room. I found that really refreshing. A lovely Italian colleague told me it was very Scottish.

Above, I joked about my pre-granny bucket list, but, in fact, I don't have any sort of bucket list. I'm pretty happy with all the things I've done in my life so far, though, if pushed, I would always say there were two things I really wanted to do and one of them was to visit the Alhambra. This was about to happen and I was immensely excited.

However, the highlight of our holiday turned out to be something completely unexpected: Cordoba and its mezquita. We had a guided tour of the former mosque, which contains a 16th century Catholic cathedral, and it just blew me away. As we reached the end, the rush of tourists became a trickle and Malcolm and I opted to stay behind and take in the magnificent building at our own pace while the others went off to be shown round the Jewish quarter.

The Alhambra, by contrast, was packed with tourists battling the early evening heat to see every part of the vast palace and fortress. Our tour was booked for 5pm, so we'd already had a long day exploring Granada and had then had to walk up the long steep hill back to our hotel. To be honest, it was quite a disappointment.

However, overall the holiday was a huge success and our guide for the week happened to be the friend of a friend who'd recommended Riviera to me on Facebook. And she was absolutely right when she said that there was plenty of free time factored into the itinerary. It was the perfect compromise. So much so that we booked another tour in June 2018, this time to the Czech Republic and Vienna to mark Malcolm's 60th birthday. On this occasion we were able to take the afternoon off and visit the Museum of Modern Art. Then, while the others were at an evening concert, we met up with a friend and colleague for drinks in a local bar.

The solution was perfect but these would be the only two tours we took, so the memories are precious.

Chapter 26

TRAVELS AND TRIBULATIONS

Meanwhile, it was back to Blighty and our weekly routine, which now included watching Grace for anything between 11 and 24 hours one day a week. She was a whirlwind.

Now, I fully appreciate that I was out of practice with young children, and Malcolm and I were still as totally inept at working baby equipment, but it's an established fact that Grace was (and still is to a certain extent) a very active child. And her speciality became hitting her head on something in the hour before we were due to deliver her home. I literally wrapped my furniture in bubble wrap for her arrival and yet she still found something hard to head-butt, just to make sure her bump was still visible for mummy and daddy when we dropped her off. Her most spectacular feat was literally gliding over the soft bean bag I'd deliberately placed in the middle of the lounge and colliding with the metal radiator. That bump literally brought her to a standstill for the rest of the day.

To keep her entertained, we found a toddler group that was held on a Monday morning where she was actually very restrained. She gained a reputation for being curious, so for puppet shows she'd be found at the back of the set trying to see how it all worked. Musicians came to play and she spent the whole time beside them watching their hands move over the instruments. She played really well with the other children, with the exception of a certain Marco, whom she never forgave for thumping her with a plastic watermelon.

She also became my fashion adviser and, before she could even talk properly, she'd monitor what I was putting on to go to toddler group and would often shake her head with a firm 'no gaggy' and point to the jacket or scarf she thought I should wear.

Gaggy was what she called her two grans and one of the first sentences she learnt was silly billy or, in her version, billy billy. "Billy billy gaggy" was her catchphrase for a while. I'd hear it as I struggled to open the highchair in a coffee shop or fold the pushchair. The evening I panicked at the tomato sauce stains on her brand-new baby-pink dungarees, she repeated "billy billy gaggy" several times, I'm sure her parents had much stronger words for me when I took her home.

The 10-mile drive back up to Kilbirnie at the end of the day was exhausting. In the dark winter nights, with fog, rain or sometimes snow, it was terrifying. I was always glad to have got her home safely and would flop on the sofa and promptly fall asleep.

Of course, once I'd recovered, I was grateful to have been able to spend time with our first grandchild and to help Iain and Lauren out with childcare, repaying in some way the support we'd had from my mum and father-in-law. But my working week had been reduced to four days and any thoughts I might have had of working while she had her afternoon nap were pipe dreams, as I inevitably nodded off on the sofa at the same time. Plus, I was doing something I hadn't actually had to do as a mother because, thanks to the childcare arrangements I'd had in place when the boys were young, I'd rarely had to liaise with clients from a swing park or with a young child in the background (did I mention how bad I am at multitasking?). As many grandparents in a similar position will know, you are the childcare and your working week shrinks.

This doesn't mean, however, that mine was all playgroups, parks and producing translations. In fact, looking back, I was extremely busy and I was doing quite a bit of travel.

As already mentioned, I negotiated the entry date to our Largs flat in April 2016 while I was at the BP16 conference in Prague. I actually gave my Newcastle presentation there to a different audience (and others who'd missed it the previous year) and went on to repeat it to several regional ITI networks. I turned it into a one-day workshop for the ITI Western Regional Group in Bristol in 2017 and was asked to talk at the annual conference of what is now the Chartered Institute of Editing and Proofreading in Lancaster in September 2018.

I was still the coordinator for the ITI Media, Arts and Tourism network and was travelling to London for the annual workshop. Plus, in 2018, the network took its own stand at the Museums & Heritage Show at Olympia.

My creative translation work had also increased and a conversation with my Italian colleague Adriana Tortoriello at one event led to us putting together a joint presentation on that topic for the 2017 ITI conference in Cardiff. I persuaded her to submit a proposal to deliver it again the following year at BP18 in Vienna and arranged a twin room for us in what turned out to be a pretty dodgy hotel. It was advertised as part of the Great Western Hotels chain and also as a boutique hotel. It turned out to be neither. The hotel chain had delisted it and it was more akin to a set from the *Addams Family* than an upmarket hotel. I was given a code to access the key to our room, as reception closed at 5pm. In other words, the family went off and left their guests to fend for themselves. When I finally managed to open the huge Austrian doors and gain entry to the badly lit premises, I had a slight problem on my hands. Our tiny, dingy room was a double, not a twin. There was a phone number for emergencies but did sharing a double bed with a colleague fall into that category? Thankfully, Adriana agreed we would make do and sort it out in the morning. We never did get our twin room because they were too busy dealing with other things, including the breakfast room ceiling partially collapsing. On day two, we arrived to see a bucket in the middle of the floor to collect the water that was dripping fairly steadily from the resultant hole. The owner was most apologetic. In fact, he was charming but totally useless.

Adriana left the day before me and when I arrived in the breakfast room on the Sunday morning, I could see there was something going on outside. 'How exciting,' I thought when I learnt we were on the Vienna marathon route. By the time I'd checked out, the race had started so I could see I'd have to let the bulk of the runners pass before I could cross the road to get to the station. I waited and waited. I eventually sat on a café terrace and ordered a drink, watching them run in the scorching heat. It was another unseasonal heatwave and they had been told not to wear fancy dress. There was only one solitary Mozart who hadn't got the memo. And I was mighty glad I had plenty of time to get to the airport because it was at least two hours before I was able to make my way unsteadily across the sea of discarded plastic cups to reach the station, which should have been a 10-minute walk from the hotel.

After a throwaway comment on Facebook back in early 2015, I had become involved with the ITI outreach project, designed to promote the translation and interpreting profession in schools, universities and to business organisations. I subsequently travelled to Portsmouth to meet with the then ITI Chair, Sara Bawa Mason, and another colleague for an initial brainstorming meeting in early 2016. We subsequently recruited a group of outreach volunteers who all finally met face-to-face three years later in Birmingham in 2019. At the ITI conference in Sheffield that year, I gave an update on what we had achieved so far.

Closer to home, I had become a regular on the Largs/Glasgow train, as I visited my mum back in Bearsden most Saturdays.

So, why am I telling you all this?

Apart from proving that I practised what I preached in my talk about CPD and marketing on a budget, I have since gained a reputation on Facebook for my travel (mis)adventures.

There have been airport evacuations. I already mentioned the bomb scare at Beauvais but there were two other airport evacuations, one because of a suspect package at Glasgow and the other a fire alarm at Prestwick. The most dramatic was probably the time I arrived at Charles de Gaulle in Paris to witness soldiers running down the up escalators blowing whistles. They told us all to leave the airport and, as I'd just arrived from the centre of the city by train, the nearest place to go was the area at the top of the escalator that led from the station. We all looked to the staff from the airport shops and cafes for guidance, but they were as clueless as we were. With a Gallic shrug, they followed us and stood in groups, lighting cigarettes.

It was about 45 minutes before we were allowed back into the airport, by which time my flight departure was getting closer. I made my way to the gate but didn't hurry because, after all, there had been a bomb scare so things wouldn't be moving fast. It turned out that my gate was at the other end of the airport, but still I didn't panic. The huge queue for security was, I reckoned, normal after a bomb scare. It wasn't until I was buying a bottle of water and heard 'Final call for Madame Huuugggueees at gate…' over the tannoy that I decided I'd better get a move on. When I reached the gate, there wasn't a soul in sight apart from the ground staff who were waiting to usher me onto the plane, which immediately began to taxi.

I sat down flustered, only to realise I recognised the lady in the next seat. She'd been at a writers' group my friend had taken me to in my capacity as project manager of the Milngavie Book & Arts Festival. I introduced myself and mentioned my friend, adding, 'I didn't think we'd take off on time after the bomb scare'. To which she replied, 'What bomb scare?' That was the day I realised just how big Charles de Gaulle airport is.

I've not had great luck travelling by train either. I've lost count of the times my train has been cancelled due to signal faults, trespassers on the line and, because the latter part of the Largs to Glasgow journey follows the coast, water hitting the electric overhead wires at Saltcoats station.

I've experienced the latter twice. Once while waiting at Saltcoats for the train back to Largs after a workshop. As the train approached, there was an almighty bang and everyone looked round to see what had happened. Had there been an explosion? No, it was just the electrics again. The passengers already on board disembarked and there then ensued a lengthy wait for a replacement bus. On the second occasion, I was actually on the train. We passed the offending section of rail and the train was engulfed by waves. 'That was fun,' I thought, until I heard the deafening bang again and we were stranded, unable to move until a train came from another line and pushed us back to Glasgow.

However, my most memorable train journey was the day I travelled to Birmingham for the outreach meeting in 2019. The Largs train was on time, so I was optimistic… until I reached Glasgow to discover there were no trains out of Central Station at all. There was a tree down on the West Coast line and, sadly, a suicide on the East Coast one. There was also a big queue of people waiting for replacement buses to Carlisle.

As I neared the top of the queue, I realised that the people in front of me hadn't been getting on buses at all but into black cabs. A Scotrail worker called out, 'Any solo travellers?' and before I knew it, I found myself in a taxi with two young lads on their way to Download Festival, a young Cambridge professor who'd been wild camping, and all their gear. It was cosy to say the least, not to mention slightly whiffy from the professor 'fresh' from the Scottish countryside. We had a great chat during the 90-minute journey but then got stuck in a long queue of what must have been a hundred black cabs trying to get into Carlisle station. The whole town was in gridlock and we couldn't get out because the cab drivers had been instructed to drop their passengers right outside the station or they wouldn't get paid. They must have reported the gridlock and all got the go-ahead to let their passengers out at the same time, as taxi doors opened almost in synchrony and a steady stream of people pulling wheeled suitcases headed towards the station... only to be met with more chaos. I finally arrived in Birmingham via a circuitous route several hours late.

Back home and at the mercy of Scotrail, I was stranded on a train in blistering heat the Saturday afternoon Troon ticket office went on fire and the whole rail system was halted. Thankfully, we were at a platform so, when the train got too hot, most of the passengers spilled outside. The local drunk (there's always at least one on a Saturday) took it upon himself to go up and down asking everyone if they were ok, cadging cigarettes at the same time.

Talking of drunks, some of the Saturday ones on the Largs train are highly entertaining, especially those I used to call the 'afternoon drunks', who would stagger onto the 5.15 at Glasgow Central, back in pre-Covid days. One girl, who was barely able to walk in sandals with huge platform soles, chose the seat opposite me (of course) beside a young guy called Mark. She spoke to Mark the whole journey and even FaceTimed her (mortified) mum, who was having a quiet early evening meal with her friend in a restaurant in Benidorm, to introduce her to her new 'train friend' and subsequently the rest of the carriage. Her plans to invite Mark to spend the Saturday evening with her were scuppered when her mum told her to phone her husband and make sure he picked her up at the station.

More recently, about 7pm on a Sunday night, a young couple boarded the train. She was carrying a very large glass of wine and it soon became apparent they'd had a few. The husband asked me if they were on the Largs train then, unprompted, told me the wine had cost £10.95, so there was no way they were going to leave it behind. Fair enough, I thought, and went back to my crossword.

When his wife fell asleep, he looked over.

'Do you need any help with your crossword?' he asked.

'I'm fine, thanks,' I said, having completed all but one clue.

Ten minutes later he asked again so, to keep him quiet, I gave him the final crossword clue: easy to remember. Six letters with a C, A, T and Y.

He puzzled for a bit then said, 'I'll phone a friend'. As he bamboozled his friend with the crossword clue, and why he was even doing someone else's crossword in the first place when his mind was far from clear, a lady who'd been sitting further back in the carriage came up as she prepared to get off at the next stop and said, 'It's catchy'.

Disappointed that she'd spoiled his fun, he hung up and turned the conversation to my suitcase.

'Do you live down this way?' he asked.

'Yes,' I said, 'I moved to Largs from Glasgow six years ago'.

'Glasgow AND Ayrshire! You've done well for yourself,' was his reply.

I just smiled and nodded.

These are the fun stories, but there have been frustrations too. Flybe changed my flight to Cardiff in 2017 and I accepted it, thinking it was a simple time change. Never in my wildest dreams would I have thought an airline could change the day too, which was my defence when I was grovelling to them two days before my original flight, having only noticed when I went to book my taxi to the airport. They put me on another flight at no extra charge.

After the ITI conference in Sheffield in 2019, I unexpectedly found myself on a replacement bus for part of the journey. Inevitably, the service was running very late when we moved back onto a train in Carlisle and the whole carriage was rooting for me to catch the last train to Largs, which I did by the skin of my teeth.

In fact, much of this travel was made possible because we'd been temporarily relieved of our grandparenting duties when Grace was joined by a little brother, Conor Mark, on 22 September 2017, and Lauren took a year's maternity leave. Of course, after that it was two for the price of one and double the trouble, but by this time Grace was at nursery and Conor was a very docile toddler.

As we approached 2020, life was good, albeit extremely busy. But we all know what happened next…

Chapter 27

LOCKED DOWN

Covid struck.

I've decided to reproduce here a post I published on LinkedIn on 8 April 2020 after the UK went into its first lockdown on 26 March, simply because it captures the raw emotion that some – if not most – of us were feeling at the time.

***

Turning 60 during an epidemic

It seemed to come out of the blue. Well, they both did actually: my 60th birthday and the Coronavirus.

The first I had planned for, with a trip to Faro in Portugal with my husband, a girls' weekend in Perthshire and meals out with friends to celebrate.

The second was happening in China, nearly 5,000 miles away, until it hit Europe. It started to feel closer at the end of March when anybody who had visited the Lombardy region in Italy (its first port of call) was told to self-isolate at home for 14 days once they arrived back in the UK. Self-isolation was a brand-new concept that shocked us – how is that possible? – and reassured us – at least we won't catch it – in equal measure.

In fact, in mid-March my translator colleagues in Lombardy had started to post on Facebook about red zones and orange zones. The first was put under lockdown and in the second, restrictions were less stringent. People were allowed to travel if they could prove it was for work or health reasons. This was major. I don't think I was alone in expecting my Italian colleagues to all come down with the virus. Fast forward one month and they have all escaped it so far, but Italy's death toll is approaching 15,000. Thankfully it now does seem to be levelling off and hopefully the country is over the worst.

The second European country to be hit was Spain, with the epicentre in Madrid. As I write this, on 8 April, the death toll there is 13,055. In France, it has topped 10,000 and in Britain, numbers are rising. Our Prime Minister, Boris Johnson, is in intensive care with the virus and several cabinet members have had it (and since recovered).

The numbers are astronomical. How can anyone get their head round announcements of 600+ deaths in a single day? Spain and France announced huge daily death tolls and we shook our heads in despair. Today, our own numbers exceeded 900. New cases are no longer relevant because so few people are being tested. The figures we are following are admissions to ICU and deaths.

As of yesterday, deaths worldwide stood at 83,090.

In the meantime, the UK has been placed under lockdown. Nurseries, schools, colleges and university buildings are closed. Teachers and lecturers are delivering lessons online. If you're not a key worker (i.e. essential for healthcare or to keep the country operational) you must work at home. If you can't work from home, you will probably have been furloughed, which means your employer can keep you on the payroll and pay you 80% of your wages (up to a limit), which will come from government funds.

Lockdown means we have to stay at home and only go out once a day for health reasons, essential shopping or exercise. We are washing our hands frequently (singing Happy Birthday twice over if we want to make sure we do it for 20 seconds), queuing to enter shops, disinfecting our shopping and all deliveries, not visiting other households (even close relatives) and staying two metres away from anyone we encounter when we leave the house.

That's the general situation in a nutshell, but everyone's individual position is different. The immediate effect on translators and interpreters has differed due to the nature of their respective jobs.

Unsurprisingly, as conferences were cancelled or postponed worldwide, interpreters found themselves with planned assignments cancelled and no work in the pipeline. Very quickly, however, companies started to plan online events and remote interpreting took off.

Some translators saw their workload disappear overnight, while others experienced no change. We work from home anyway, so how much could our lives change? Quite a bit as it happens.

I continued to receive work initially but routine – and concentration – went out the window from day one. My life had been pretty busy, actually much busier than I had realised, and suddenly I have permission to stop. We can't look after the grandkids on a Wednesday, I can't visit my mum on a Saturday, it's not a great idea to continue my weekly Sunday walks with my husband, so I have all this time on my hands.

But…

… so much needs cleaning: carpets, kitchen cupboard doors, the oven, the tile grouting in the bathroom.

… so much needs planning in advance, not least meals and shopping:

I have autoimmune diseases so, although not instructed to stay at home, my one shopping trip to Morrisons had me hyperventilating. Outside, people generally adhere to the two-metre rule but once inside a supermarket they see what they need on the shelf and push in to get it. Our store is small, so marking out queuing positions two metres apart means you are queuing in the aisles and people need to get past.

Sainsbury's put me on their vulnerable list for delivery slots, for which I am eternally grateful, but my shopping habits have gone from a weekly shop, with regular top-ups and visits to local shops, to a weekly delivery and avoiding the shops completely in between. Not easy when items are disappearing from your virtual shopping basket as fast as you're putting them in.

… there's so much continuing professional development I could do:

- French films are available online for free
- FNAC has made all its audiobooks free to download
- there are free online courses aplenty
- French colleagues are posting regular updates in French I could read
- I have a backlog of Decanter magazines to get through
- I haven't read Marie France online, which I promised myself I would do when I stopped my subscription

… there are so many online exercise options:
- my weekly yoga class has now gone virtual
- Oti Mabusi of Strictly Come Dancing fame is giving daily dance classes
- other options that I won't even consider because I know I'll do myself an injury

… so many films and TV programmes to catch up on:

- a list of food-related movies everyone should see during lockdown
- daytime programmes I don't normally give myself permission to watch
- Tiger King, aka Joe Exotic, on Netflix

… so much cooking I want to do:

- I want to bake a cake since watching celebrity Bake-Off on TV last night
- I want to try some of the fabulous recipes that local chefs and Paris Gluten Free cafes have been demonstrating online
- I want to work my way through all the exotic ingredients I've filled my cupboards with over the years: chai seeds, sumac, Medjool dates, ground flaxseed…
- I want to remember to take something out of the freezer for tonight's dinner

… so many books I want to read:

- a whole shelf from a book subscription I stopped because I was finding them too heavy. Maybe I'll get into them now that I have the time?
- a book I asked my son to give me for Christmas (21 Lessons for the 21st Century, published last year but of course completely out of date now)
- a book about tea I bought on a whim on a visit to the Louis Vuitton Foundation earlier this year

So much, so many options, kindly made available for free to stop us getting bored. But I'm not bored and I don't think I will be for a long time.

Instead, my days go something like this:

- get up late(ish) and have a leisurely breakfast as I watch the morning news (and worry) and catch up on Facebook (trying to only read the positive posts),
- try to do something constructive before stopping at 11.45 for my daily 20 minutes yoga practice,
- watch the Scottish update at 12.30 (worry and completely undo the calm I had achieved during the practice)
- watch the lunchtime news headlines in case I've missed anything
- watch an episode of Joe Exotic with my husband (the one hour we spend together each day before disappearing into our unnecessary self-isolation again thanks to being a two-TV household)
- go for a walk, spending the whole time trying to stay two metres away from everybody else
- watch my favourite programme – Escape to the Chateau DIY – at 4pm
- realise I've forgotten to take something out of the freezer for dinner (again)
- …

Of course, some days are better. I might have some work to do. I might manage a yoga practice, a walk and an online dance class. I might actually remember to organise dinner and spend a little time in the kitchen preparing something nice. The sun might be shining, so I might watch Escape to the Chateau from the balcony.

Other days some things just don't happen. Today I abandoned my yoga practice and can't be bothered going for a walk, but I sat down to write a chapter of this book.

Other days there are endless phone calls, messages and the daily FaceTime conversation with the grandkids and before I know it, I've done nothing else.

When I think back, my initial reaction was complete exhaustion. My weeks had been pretty hectic. I had had a lot of work and since the start of the year had often been putting in some hours at weekends to free me up to look after the grandkids on a Wednesday. Sometimes, depending on Iain's shift, we would have them from around 4pm on Tuesday till 6pm on a Wednesday. They live 10 miles away, so I was driving up and down the road to collect them, do nursery drop-offs and pick-ups, and then take them home again.

There was also an element of nervous exhaustion. Before lockdown began, everyone was concerned. The UK was being told by other countries that it wasn't acting fast enough and all we could do was watch the virus take hold elsewhere and carry on as normal. We were worried about ourselves but also about our families.

When lockdown was announced, everything and everyone seemed to come to a standstill. Some translators suddenly stopped getting any work at all and started posting on Facebook about their lockdown projects, parents went into home-schooling overdrive and foodie translators were spending hours in their kitchens cooking and baking.

And there was little old me, still slogging away at the computer. I was eternally grateful for the work, essentially being sent by an agency that was winding down the financial season, but I too wanted to cook, work on the house, read books, watch films and do so much more.

Imagine my surprise when one Monday morning, nearly one week into lockdown, my work dried up and I didn't know what to do. I just sat on the sofa looking out the window at our gorgeous view and procrastinated. In between procrastinating, I read Facebook and Twitter and fell asleep.

Admittedly, I had already been cancelling events and staying indoors for over two weeks because I had developed a cough. I was pretty sure the cough wasn't Coronavirus, as it didn't fit the description, and I had a horrible dry throat and chest, which is a fairly normal Sjogren's Syndrome symptom. I had continued to work on and look after the kids while feeling pretty awful. Although I'm fairly good at looking after myself at the best of times, that usually means not doing things I didn't have to do. What I had been doing were things I needed to do.

So I just gave in and didn't feel guilty. I tried to do yoga but my body ached afterwards, so I stopped doing that. I didn't go out for walks because I couldn't be 100% sure it wasn't the virus, so I let myself stare out the window, watch rubbish TV, nap and get my strength back. I didn't feel overwhelmed. That feeling kicked in this week.

When the cough finally stopped, and I felt better physically, there was another surprise in store. When there's a deadly virus going about and you have one of the symptoms, your focus is inevitably on yourself. Is it better or worse today? Do I have a temperature? Maybe it's not my Sjogren's Syndrome? That's pretty time-consuming and emotionally draining. The relief of getting rid of my cough gave way to a surge of emotions.

I can be sitting happily looking out of the window, enjoying filling my lungs with sea air on a walk or happily cooking away in the kitchen and I'll suddenly burst into tears. I'm doing it again as I write this paragraph. As someone who's not usually very emotional, it has really taken me aback. Of course there are also the happy tears after a good news story on the TV, the acts of kindness being shown in the community and a beautiful smile from the grandkids on FaceTime, but these moments of grief were completely alien to me.

Through keeping in touch with colleagues on Facebook and talking to friends and family on the phone, I know I'm not alone. In fact, several articles I've read have told me it's grief I'm feeling. Everyone is grieving the life they can no longer have. But how can we grieve at missing out on trips, visiting family or ordering takeaways when so many people are grieving the loss of loved ones? That can't be right. Surely, we are not as shallow and self-centred as that? It seems it's because these are things we can personally feel and comprehend when the numbers of people dying and falling seriously ill are way beyond our comprehension, something we've never experienced first-hand before.

There was also a useful article posted by an academic who had lived in war-torn countries, warning people to stop. To give up the idea of writing that article you've been meaning to write, of becoming the best home-school teacher in the country, of throwing yourself headlong into marketing as soon as work dries up. To simply stop and give yourself time to adjust. Wise words.

And there are many more among the gloom and doom. Some days we appreciate them and take them on board, other days they seem empty and shallow and don't make a difference. Some days are just very dark and we need to accept them and hope the next day will be better.

And for me it usually is. For others, especially those people who suffer from mental health problems, it might not be. So I feel grateful and make the most of the day ahead. I can cope with one achievement, no matter how small, every day but what about perfectionists? What about those people who push themselves too hard? I just hope that, through time, the pressure on people, especially young mums and women hitting 60, to be perfect and achieve amazing things, might pale a little. Let's face it, at the end of the lockdown, beautiful hair will be a thing of the past. No access to hairdressers will be one of the levelling factors of this virus.

But back to my birthday. I know I'm an adult and can deal with the fact my 60th birthday is going to be spent in lockdown. I know I'm lucky to be able to afford a bottle of bubbly and some nice food to share with my husband. I know a lot of the meals I've had to cancel can probably be rearranged once this is all over (and restaurants don't have waiting lists the length of The Ivy's). I know the holiday in Portugal can be rearranged (provided the airline and hotel are still in business). I know my friend turns 60 next year and will be celebrating her birthday with her friends in Portugal too, so I will still get the chance to discover the country. But I can't help feeling a bit disappointed at having had to cancel so many trips, including one to a Kent wine estate that was a birthday present to a friend who turned 60 last December. And OK I admit that I was hoping for a better 60th birthday because my father-in-law was diagnosed with lung cancer on the day of my 50th.

According to an article I read, we are allowed to acknowledge our disappointment too, so there you go. I've done it. It's not by any means taking over my life. When my elder son asked me what I wanted for my birthday, I said, honestly, I just wanted everyone I knew to be well and stay well. Birthday celebrations can be rearranged.

***

Isn't hindsight amazing? Look at the numbers of cases reported at the beginning and the optimism that Italy was on its way out of the pandemic. In fact, you've probably already spotted that the title of my post calls it an epidemic because it wasn't until later that Covid was declared a pandemic. Many colleagues, mainly women with young families, thanked me for writing such an honest account, as they really thought that other women were baking banana bread and in the throes of becoming a yoga goddess while they struggled to keep working and home-school their children.

This was far from the case, despite reports on social media. On the plus side, communities were coming together and looking after the most vulnerable who'd been told to 'shield', a new term for stay at home and avoid contact with the outside world. Every Thursday night, people would go outside their front doors or onto their balconies to clap and show support for all the NHS doctors and nurses and other key workers who were keeping the country going.

However, all contact with loved ones was stopped, so we didn't see the family for some weeks. Then, when restrictions began to ease in the summer of 2020, we were allowed to meet up outside and one incident sticks in my mind. On this particular day, we had gone up to Kilbirnie to go for a walk with Iain, Grace and Conor. We were keeping our distance when suddenly I felt something brush my hand. Grace had sneaked up close and was hinting that she wanted to hold it. On the premise that we weren't indoors and I had antiseptic gel in my pocket I followed the cue and took hold of hers. She'd obviously been told she couldn't go near us or touch us so, to absolve herself of all guilt, she said, 'Dad, gran took my hand'. I can scarcely believe that we were in that situation and often wonder how the pandemic will have marked the little ones who lived through it with us.

  And, of course, the restrictions were necessary because people were dying every day without their loved ones by their side. And these loved ones were having to grieve with only virtual support from family and friends. Little did I know at this point that I would be in a similar situation one year later.

Chapter 28

LETTING GO

When we went to Edinburgh in August 2020 to celebrate Malcolm's 62nd birthday there were signs that his health was not good. He was struggling to walk very far, so, at his suggestion, we cut our trip short. I thought it was because there was so little open in the city itself – a far cry from the usual buzzing Edinburgh during the Festival and Fringe – and that did play a part, but looking back I realise he was in a lot of pain. He'd suffered from swelling in his knees and foot for many years and had been told it was either gout or arthritis, a consequence of the regular soakings he took while working as a postman. He insisted on treating it with Ibuprofen, which, in fairness, usually did the trick and the swelling would subside after a few days. However, latterly the bouts were becoming more frequent and incapacitating.

It settled slightly again once we got home from Edinburgh but recurred several more times until, one day in December, he found himself barely able to walk. He finally agreed to contact his GP, who asked him to come into the surgery and immediately sent him to hospital for tests and a scan.

Covid restrictions meant I couldn't go in with him, so I dropped him off and waited in the freezing car in the car park looking out over the snowy hills. After what seemed like hours, he finally came out with a diagnosis of cellulitis, a very painful infection of the skin. His leg had been scanned to rule out a DVT and he had been prescribed blood-thinning medication until it was checked again a week later. He was also given antibiotics for the infection.

A further scan the following week indicated there was no DVT present, so he was told he could stop the blood thinners. He was also warned it could take six weeks before he saw some improvement. For someone who could boast he had never had a headache in his life, this was devastating news. He was miserable.

Christmas 2020 duly arrived and, as for every other family in the UK, it was pretty low-key because Covid numbers were increasing again. A planned easing of restrictions over a five-day period was subsequently revised to Christmas Day only, with a limit of eight people from three households allowed to get together. Matthew came home to spend it with us and stayed on when the country went into lockdown on Boxing Day.

Then, on 1st January 2021, the UK officially left the European Union. The country had voted in favour of the move on 23 June 2016 and the long, drawn-out negotiations began to be implemented. This did nothing to help an economy that was already suffering the effects of Covid. My work was trickling in but certainly showing no signs of picking up any time soon. The outlook for my business was pretty bleak, and I know I wasn't alone, but little did I know that would soon be the least of my worries.

On the afternoon of 5 February 2022 my life changed forever. At around 1pm, Malcolm went out to get the local bus to town. Just before it arrived, he felt unwell but boarded it anyway. However, it was soon evident that he was pretty ill and, when the bus arrived in town, the driver sought help from the pharmacist at the local supermarket who brought Malcolm home in his car. He suggested he might have an infection, but I realised immediately that there was something badly wrong. This was at 2.10 pm.

We called for an ambulance and waited in the communal hallway, as Malcolm was too ill to climb the three flights of stairs and Covid restrictions meant we couldn't go into a neighbour's flat. The pharmacist had to get back to the shop, so he called in a member of the Largs Community Resilience Team to stay with us. At this point, Malcolm was struggling to breathe and I knew it was his leg. He had a DVT.

We called to chase up the ambulance, but we also happened to be in the middle of a storm. Roads were closed and a railway embankment had collapsed. To add to the drama, there had been a fatal stabbing outside the hospital the previous evening and the place was awash with press. Ambulances were struggling to get in and out of the grounds.

Finally, a paramedic arrived to do advance first aid and put Malcolm on oxygen, but he suddenly keeled over. The paramedic realised he'd had a heart attack and started CPR. It was at least another 40 minutes before the ambulance crew finally arrived at 5.20pm. They managed to get a slight heartbeat, but I was told not to hold out hope. Minutes later, the paramedics came back to tell us he had died in the ambulance before it even set off for the hospital.

Thankfully, Matthew was with me at the flat and I'd been liaising with Iain, who decided there was nothing he could do that evening and would come down the following day. And Covid restrictions meant none of my other family members could visit. In fact, even if they'd been tempted to bend the rules, one of them tested positive the following day and others had to self-isolate for 10 days, as they'd been close contacts.

Now, if I can be permitted a touch of dark humour, what happened later that evening was quite surreal. I answered the buzzer to find two local policemen at the door. They'd been sent to ask some questions and do a report because the death had occurred outside the home. One was very tall and the other was extremely short and wearing a snorkelling mask (minus the tube) to protect himself from Covid, I presume. He looked like a Minion.

I'll be kind to them and surmise they hadn't been asked to follow up a death before because they conducted it like a murder investigation. They were asking all sorts of totally irrelevant questions, like where Malcolm and I had met, when we got married, etc. They also interviewed Matthew as though he was suspect number 2 before the Minion went off to take photos of 'the scene'. His taller counterpart then started to receive messages on his radio. There was a suspicious-looking guy with a dog wandering the streets of Largs. He was struggling to work out what to do about what could in fact easily have been just a dog walker dressed for the wind and rain when he received another call, this time from someone at the morgue. They were anxious to know if we'd arranged a funeral director.

It all became too much for him to handle, so he left us in peace to find his colleague. Matthew and I looked at each other in disbelief. 'Did that just happen?' I asked, as I poured us each a brandy in the vain hope it would help us sleep. It didn't.

The next day, Lauren dropped Iain off at the flat before going to collect Grace and Conor, who'd been with their other grandparents on the Friday afternoon and stayed there overnight. She had the unenviable task of breaking the news to them that their grandad had died. Conor was still too young to understand, but Grace was heartbroken. Nevertheless, from the depths of her uncontrollable sobs she blurted out, 'Will gran have to get another boyfriend now?' Even in the darkest moments she can make us laugh.

I'd been trying to let as many people know about Malcolm's death since early morning and, as fast as I was contacting them, other people were phoning or messaging because they'd heard the news through another channel. For those I couldn't contact directly, I put a post on Facebook and was totally overwhelmed by the response. I'm connected to a lot of translator friends through the site and this was when I truly realised that translation and interpreting is more than an industry; it's one big global community.

Iain took over the funeral arrangements and, as Malcolm wasn't religious, requested a humanist celebrant. But first there had to be a post-mortem, which didn't happen for another two weeks.

In the meantime, the flat filled with bouquet after bouquet of beautiful flowers and thoughtful cards and messages as we put together a service to celebrate Malcolm's life. Music had always played a big part, so it was chosen with care. He had Welsh roots and was a Tom Jones fan, so *Green, Green Grass of Home* was a must. We showed a photomontage to Bowie's *Where Are We Now?* after Iain told our Berlin story in his eulogy, and the final piece was *To Love Somebody* by the Bee Gees, in memory of him blasting Bee Gees songs through the house most Saturday nights.

As we pieced together his life, helped by a lovely letter from a friend who filled in the gaps of his early years, it became evident that Babybel cheese would have to get a mention. Why? Because grandad was always being accused of eating the stock I kept for Grace and Conor. One Saturday I'd met Iain and the children on the train to Glasgow by chance and Grace asked, 'What's grandad doing?' When I replied 'Just the usual', she came back quick as a flash with 'On the computer and eating all the Babybels, then'.

The night of the funeral my Facebook friends raised a glass to Malcolm and ate a Babybel in his memory.

There had been nine close family members at the crematorium and afterwards we all went our separate ways, unable to share even a cup of tea due to Covid restrictions. I was so grateful for modern technology, which enabled so many friends and family to join us virtually, but just over an hour after Matthew and I had left for the crematorium, we found ourselves back at the flat, not quite sure what to do next.

Indeed, the 'not quite sure what to do next' extended to my life because every single aspect of it was going to change. When my dad died, I was obviously devastated and grieved for some time, but my main focus was supporting my mum. When I wasn't with her, my life continued pretty much as normal. This is far from the case when you lose a partner, and Malcolm and I had been together for 36 years.

When I woke in the morning, it would immediately hit me that he was no longer there. On good days I might be getting along fine and then be stopped in my tracks by something totally out of the blue. In the supermarket, it might be the things I used to buy for him, which I no longer needed to put in my basket. At home, it might be a programme on the

TV or a song on the radio. There were constant reminders, some comforting and others heartbreaking. Initially, the intensity was unbearable, but very gradually it began to subside as the Covid restrictions eased at the end of April 2020 and I was able to meet up with friends and family in person again.

Workwise, I had been in the very fortunate position that I could take time off when Malcolm died. Financially, this was possible thanks to a critical illness policy with death cover I had taken out for myself and my family when I embarked on my freelance career back in 1997. Indeed, although it was an outgoing I could ill afford in the early years, it should definitely have featured on my list of non-negotiable expenses in my Newcastle talk. The money bought me both time and a much-needed new bathroom. In retrospect, the latter was possibly a little extravagant, but it became my haven, and a lengthy soak in the bath on difficult days helped me immensely.

My clients were understanding and very patient, either waiting for me or passing work on to colleagues I recommended. One small agency checked in regularly and ended each email with reassurances that I could take as long as I liked, as they would never replace me. A small gesture, but it meant so much.

I probably took six weeks off before I gradually started easing myself back in by accepting small translations from clients. I wanted to be absolutely sure I could still deliver the quality they expected and wouldn't let them down. While some days I would have been more than able to do that, there were still some tough situations to handle that could momentarily set me back.

Dealing with the death of a loved one is very personal. Some friends told me they had sought solace in their work, which is equally valid if that's what helped them. But I know that stress of any sort makes me physically ill, so I always do my utmost to avoid it at any cost.

I keep my workload manageable and rarely work evenings or weekends. I never overload my social diary either and if it gets too packed, I factor in a quiet spell afterwards to help me recover. I also get easily overstimulated and it can take me a long while to wind down after a trip or a night out.

I had always thought that it was some quirk of my Sjögren's syndrome that I was sensitive to so many outside stimuli and was so easily overwhelmed, and then I discovered Elaine N. Aron's book *The Highly Sensitive Person*. I immediately recognised myself and read the book cover to cover in one sitting.

Many of you who know me well might be quite surprised at this, especially if you're aware of my packed travel itinerary in early 2022 when, it seems, every event that had been postponed because of Covid happened one after another.

The fact is, over the years I have developed a switch-off mechanism that helps me cope. If things become too much for me, I can usually focus on the present to stop myself from stressing. However, after Malcolm died it malfunctioned.

For the first few weeks I had panic attacks and I found it especially difficult to drive past the crematorium. Even a trip into town could be a challenge. The attacks were mild, thankfully – and CBD oil proved to be my saviour – but initially very debilitating. Physically, my body also took a blow and I didn't have the strength to continue my yoga classes. The weekly breathing and relaxation classes my yoga teacher had introduced into her programme during Covid were, on the other hand, a godsend.

During this time, Matthew was still here. He stayed with me until lockdown restrictions eased at the end of April and he could travel back to his flat in Glasgow. I was extremely grateful for his company, but by this point we both knew that we needed our own space again. My life was slowly beginning to move forward and, looking back, I think that time I had to spend alone helped me come to terms with my loss. There was no escaping the grief because there were no distractions. Nobody could visit or invite me to stay so, with the immense help of my family and friends, albeit virtually, I worked my way through the process and by the time summer arrived I felt ready to move on.

But what lay ahead?

Chapter 29

AND STARTING OVER

Grace, then aged 5, was still struggling to understand what had happened to her grandad. She had so many questions and the first time I drove her and Conor down to Largs after Malcolm's death, I was barraged from the back seat of the car:

'I just don't understand how grandad died,' she began.

I tried to keep it simple with 'He had a sore leg, Grace, and that made him very ill.'

'But how do you die from a sore leg? Did he not go to the doctor? Did you go with him to hospital?'

When I explained that he hadn't gone to hospital, her focus turned to how I looked after him at the bottom of the stairs.

'Did you put a blanket over him? What sort of blanket do you put over a dying man?'

Before I could think of an answer, we were driving past the crematorium and she asked, 'Is that where you had grandad's funeral?'

'Yes,' I replied.

'How many people were there? Did you put up decorations? What did you do with the body?'

This last question was a tricky one, but I thought it best to be honest.

'It was burned, Grace.'

Silence.

'But why did you do that? How will we be able to visit his grave?'

As I was explaining the concept of ashes, she suddenly hit me with 'You know, if you get a new boyfriend, I'm still going to talk about grandad.'

'I can assure you, Grace, I'm not thinking about getting a new boyfriend,' I replied.

'How old are you anyway?' she asked.

'I'm nearly 61…' I started to say before she came in with 'Holy Moly, how old can you be to have a new boyfriend?'

My tears turned to hysterical laughter. Who knows, maybe one day I'll be able to answer that question?

When I could turn my attention back to work, I realised the majority of my clients were in industries that had been hit hard by Covid and Brexit, which had a knock-on effect for my business. True to form, I decided that maybe I needed a change anyway. Perhaps I could flip houses, upcycle furniture or get a job in the local gin and chocolate shop? The latter option particularly appealed.

It was round about this time that I saw an advert for a part-time job that was well paid and would, I thought, be perfect for me. Millport Town Hall, on the island of Cumbrae, a short 10-minute ferry trip from Largs, was being refurbished and was looking for a community liaison officer to develop it as a hub for local groups and businesses. I had experience building communities, organising events, coordinating networks and more through my voluntary work with the ITI and project-managing the Milngavie Book & Arts Festival. Maybe this was meant to be?

It wasn't. I didn't even get an interview. I was initially disappointed, as the regular salary would have given me security, but going through the application process made me realise that I'd put a lot of time and effort into building my business and it's what I'm good at. Changing course would have been an easier, short-term solution but ultimately not the answer.

It's perhaps not unnatural to want a complete change after a major life event, but I decided at that point that I would make no major decisions for at least a year. Instead, I've focussed on rebuilding my life in Largs. I volunteer at the food bank, have taken a course on upcycling furniture and also took myself along to a dance class that was advertised on the local Facebook page. I was particularly excited about learning the West Coast Swing, but the 'teacher' didn't want to teach, which didn't bode well, and he frustrated us all with his improvisation. The class folded after only a few weeks. Not everything has gone to plan, but it's been good fun trying.

Grace and Conor are now 7 and 4, so my duties are limited to a school and nursery pick-up most Wednesdays. This has helped me reclaim some of my working week, and my Facebook friends eagerly await the latest instalment of their back-of-the-car conversations.

Recently, as we approached Kilbirnie on the drive home from Largs, Grace said:

'Conor, there's a whole city over there. Looking at it you can understand how the earth is round.'

To which Conor replied: 'But we need to know where it ends, Grace.'

These two little people really have been a ray of sunshine in difficult times and Grace seems to be coming to terms with her grandad's death. Only a week ago, as we drove past the crematorium, she said:

'I wonder how grandad is getting on "up there". I tell you something, there are no beds.'

'Why not?' I asked, somewhat puzzled.

235

'Because ghosts are light, so they can sleep on the clouds.'

You heard it here first.

My road back to normality has not all been plain sailing. My 89-year-old mum was admitted to hospital when she took seriously ill after a fall back in November 2021. After a lengthy hospital stay and respite care, we finally settled her into a home at the end of February this year. It has been a long, emotional journey, with Covid restrictions on visiting, a further serious fall and late-night emergency admissions. Her dementia has also worsened as a result. Experiencing the sudden death of a loved one is hard, but witnessing the slow decline of someone in old age is not any easier. A salutary lesson that you really do have to live your best possible life while you can.

And to prove my point, I recently had a VIP tour of Gusbourne wine estate in Kent with some close friends. The sun was shining, the wine was flowing and the food was delicious. A day to remember, even if some of my recollection is slightly hazy, and a great way to kick-start my CPD year.

This was closely followed by the first in-person ITI conference since 2019, which was held in Brighton on 31st May and 1st June. When the theme – Embracing change, emerging stronger – was announced, I did briefly consider submitting a proposal. After all, I'd experienced my fair share of change over the last two years and I do believe I have emerged stronger. But it was too soon. The emotion of seeing so many friends and colleagues again after such a long time was quite overwhelming, so I was pleased to be able to sit back and enjoy the talks.

Armed with some useful tips and inspired by the infectious enthusiasm and optimism about the future of the translation and interpreting industry, I feel it's time for me to focus on my business again. I've overcome hurdles before, so I'm confident I can do it again.

Besides, when one colleague in Brighton asked me what I had done when work was slow, I had a ready answer for her.

I wrote a book.

EPILOGUE

I've come to the end of the book but certainly not the end of my journey. I don't know what lies ahead, or what life might throw at me next, but what I do know is that I'm happy I've done what I can in most situations, been proactive as well as reactive, and worked my way through some pretty major life events… and I've learnt a lot along the way.

It was interesting to look back on my freelance career and analyse it after 25 years. I suspected, and now know for sure, that I'm not, and never will be, goal-orientated. But that doesn't mean that I'm not strategic. I generally have a good idea of where I'm going (unless I'm in a car) and keep my eyes open en route.

In concrete terms, I've never had a five-year plan (or any plan for that matter), audited my business, set myself objectives or tracked my progress. These are all very valid, highly recommended even, if you want to get to the top of your game. They're just not for me. I prefer to keep my business head on at all times and seize opportunities. And, by far, the best things I've done are networking with colleagues, keeping up my French to be able to communicate fluently with direct clients and – possibly – choosing to focus on a single language. I say possibly because my workload during Covid might have been higher if

I'd had more than French to offer, but it's the route I chose early on in my freelance career and there's no going back now.

This is the approach that works for me, but it doesn't mean it will work for you. We all have to find our own way. To use another cliché, for me it's been a marathon, not a sprint, and I have one final anecdote to illustrate this point.

There is a particular chain of referrals that began back at the 2012 BP translators' conference in Budapest. Nothing actually happened for two years, then I was contacted for one small job which led to another bigger job, which led to more regular work and then the French to English translation of the website of a colleague who works in the opposite direction from me. The final link in the chain (so far) has been with a prestigious direct client in Paris. Proof that every single contact you make is important because you never know where it might ultimately take you. And it won't always happen right away.

On a personal note, the last eighteen months have been far from easy, but with the amazing support of family, friends and colleagues I have got through them and am now in the process of rebuilding my life. I'm also discovering that Largs is the perfect place to do this. It's a beautiful town famous for its ice-cream and fish and chips, but there are so many other good reasons to live here. First and foremost, I love being beside the sea. There's nothing nicer than taking a stroll along the front to clear your head after a long session on the computer. It's also a very sociable town and I've met some great, like-minded people and taken up new hobbies.

There are downsides, of course. Trains to Glasgow are hourly and can be pretty unreliable. The roads are often closed for one reason or another and diversions can be 30 miles. But life itself is full of diversions, one of which brought me down to the Ayrshire coast where I can now spend time with my beautiful, bonkers, and very loving, grandchildren.

Life happens and things change but for as long as I live in this flat on the scenic west coast of Scotland, I will always have a grandstand view of the sunsets. Days come and go, some are better than others, but in the wise words of American essayist Ralph Waldo Emerson:

Every sunset brings the promise of a new dawn

About the author

Alison Hughes is a French to English freelance translator for the creative industries. She worked for 16 years in the wine and spirits industry before going freelance in 1997. She now lives in Largs, on the beautiful west coast of Scotland.

For further information visit:
alison@alisonhughes-translations.co.uk

Follow her on Twitter: @AHcreattrans

Or connect on Linkedin:
www.linkedin.com/in/AHcreattrans

Printed in Great Britain
by Amazon

85850982R00139